Funny Animals and More

Other Books by Fred Patten

Watching Anime, Reading Manga: 25 Years of Essays and Reviews (2004)

Edited by Fred Patten:

Best in Show: Fifteen Years of Outstanding Furry Fiction (2003)
reprinted as: *Furry!; The World's Best Anthropomorphic Fiction!* (2006)

Already Among Us: An Anthropomorphic Anthology (2012)

The Ursa Major Awards Anthology: A Tenth Anniversary Celebration (2012)

What Happens Next: An Anthology of Sequels (2013)

Five Furry Fortunes (2014)

Funny Animals and More
FROM ANIME TO ZOOMORPHICS

Fred Patten

Theme Park Press

Theme Park Press publishes its books in a variety of print and electronic formats. Some content that appears in one format may not appear in another.

Editor: Bob McLain
Layout: Artisanal Text
Cover Design: Dan Cunningham

ISBN 978-1-941500-00-2
10 9 8 7 6 5 4 3 2 1
Printed in the United States of America

Theme Park Press | www.ThemeParkPress.com
Address queries to bob@themeparkpress.com

For Bob Konikow, and the gang of animation professionals and fans (and occasional guests like Bob Clampett and Frank Tashlin) who gathered at his house in Los Angeles around 1970 for informal weekly screenings of cartoon shorts and theatrical features (including Jack Warner's personal print of Coal Black and de Sebben Dwarfs, *which we showed almost every week). This is where I first saw many rarities such as Disney's* Victory Through Air Power *in the days before video tapes and DVDs, and where I first felt welcomed into animation fandom's "inner circle".*

Thank you!

Contents

Foreword

Fred Patten has been a friend and colleague of mine for over 30 years, a respected comics and anime historian, and a significant part of the pioneering "first fandom" of comic book and animation enthusiasts, without whom today's mega Comic Cons, comics shops, and Hollywood's current comic-book fixation would probably not exist.

Fred Patten knows a thing or two about international comics, print cartoons, and animation. In fact, he knows more those subjects than anyone else I know; his deep interest in science fiction and animation has led him to explore the whole world of fantasy media—literally, from Europe, Asia, and South America, and with animation now emerging in India and Africa, Fred is already ahead of the pack in documenting that work.

He is best known for his research and writings regarding anime. I dare say he might have been the first U.S. citizen to recognize the growing art and artistry of Japanese animation—in the 1970s—and then write about it for English-speaking readers.

Fred and I became pen-pals back then in the 1970s (back in the days of pens, paper, and communication through the mail service) and later wrote (separately) for some of the same fanzines and professional publications. His stewardship of the California-based Cartoon/Fantasy Organization (C/FO) was legendary on the East coast (where I was based then)—and we were quite jealous of all the goodies Fred was screening out there in Los Angeles.

With Fred's blessing I helped organize a C/FO-NY in the 1980s, which brought together fans (and some professionals) of anime past and present. When I moved to L.A. in the late 1980s, and co-founded (with Carl Macek) a company called Streamline Pictures to distribute anime films to theatres and video), Fred was the first and only person we hired to help us run the operation. His knowledge of anime was invaluable.

Fred was a contributing writer to two of my book projects, *Animation Art* (2004) and *The Animated Movie Guide* (2005), overseeing the anime sections of both books. His professionalism and expertise were an important part in making those books successful—and his contributions, based on feedback from educators and enthusiasts who've used the books, were particularly vital.

To say Fred is a resource and a treasure would be an understatement. He has been an important link between those who create the works and those who consume and enjoy them.

So it was a no-brainer that Fred was one of the first people I enlisted as a contributor to my revitalized Cartoon Research blog. One of the goals of my blog was to not only to post about unknown and obscure pieces of animation history, but to give several knowledgeable friends—who, like Fred, had not taken the plunge online with their own blogs—a place to let loose with information they have gathered for many years and had yet to share with interested, like-minded readers.

Jerry Beck
Animation Historian
CartoonResearch.com
March 2014

Introduction

I have been an animation enthusiast for all my life, and an animation scholar, writing articles about it, for over thirty years. I co-founded the Cartoon/Fantasy Organization, the first American fan club for Japanese anime, in May 1977 (it's still meeting), and I have written so much about anime that I have developed a reputation as being interested in that field only. I edited the best of my articles on anime into a book that is still selling nine years later, as an e-book after the trade paperback edition sold out: *Watching Anime, Reading Manga: 25 Years of Essays and Reviews* (Stone Bridge Press, September 2004). But my interest has always been in animation without limits.

In early March 2013, Jerry Beck invited me to write a weekly column for his Cartoon Research website ("Dedicated to Classic Cartoons: Past, Present & Future"). My first "Funny Animals and More" column appeared on March 14. I was 31 columns and over 55,000 words into it when Jim Korkis, another Cartoon Research columnist, gave me the idea of using my "Funny Animals and More" columns as the basis for a book.

I have continued to write my column each week, and some of these later columns will be used as the basis for more books once there is enough material to fill them.

In many cases, I have continued to learn more about my weekly topics after the columns have been posted online. I have added the new information to the content in this book, so it is more complete and more up-to-date than my original columns.

Particular thanks are owed to Vinnie Bartalucci, DBenson, Charles Brubaker, John Paul Cassidy, Dwight Decker, Patrick Drazen, Eric Graf, Jim Korkis, Nic Kramer, Alain Mendez, Alfons Moline, Justin Mullis, Jay Pennington, Chris Peterson, Gilles Poitras, Poptique, Dan Riba, Steve Segal, Scott Shaw!, Chris Sobieniak, and Tony.

Here it is. I hope that you enjoy reading it as much as I have enjoyed writing it.

Fred Patten
North Hollywood, CA
March 2014

My weekly column on Cartoon Research usually contains weblinks to video samples that could not be included in this book. If you want to see the videos, go to http://cartoonresearch.com. The rest of Cartoon Research is well worth reading, too.

America Discovers Anime

How Home Video Created Anime Fandom

In April 1993, UCLA's Animation Workshop hosted a birthday party for animation veteran Walter Lantz, then 94 years old. (I think it was at this party that Lantz announced that he had recently found his birth certificate, and was shocked to learn that he was a year older than he had always thought. He was born in 1899, not 1900 as his parents had told him.) Lantz was wheelchair-bound and very weak, but his mind was still sharp. He died the next March, just before the Animation Workshop could hold a 1994 birthday party for him.

Someone at that 1993 party asked Lantz, who worked on his first cartoon in 1915 and directed his first cartoon in 1924, what he thought had been the greatest technological development in the history of animation. The addition of sound to silent cartoons? The multiplane camera? The replacement of hand cel coloring by computer coloring? Lantz surprised everyone by insisting that it was the introduction of home VCRs in 1975.

I don't know if he was recorded, but he said approximately:

> In 1975 animation was a dying art! All the theatrical animation studios were closed except for Disney, and by 1975 even Disney was moribund. Animation for TV was all toy and cereal commercials, and was so bland that nobody but little children watched it. The very few festivals of animation were glorifications of the past, attended mostly by animation veterans and cinematic scholars, not the public. Then, in 1975, the first home video cassette recorders came out. They took about a decade to become widespread, but suddenly the public was asking TV stations to show more classic cartoons so they could record them to watch whenever they wanted. Movie studios and whoever owned the rights to old cartoons found that there was big money in putting them out on video. The first video releases of old prints were later upgraded to remastered prints with original title cards. Today, new animation features are being made because the studios know that they can make as much or more from video sales

as from theatrical screenings. Animation that hasn't been seen in decades is available again, and permanently for whenever anyone wants to see it, not just when its studio re-releases it theatrically or on TV. The animation industry was just short of dying when the first VCRs came out; now it's bigger than ever!

Before the Christmas season of 1975, about the only VCR available was Sony's U-matic, and that was only introduced in 1971. It was bought in the cinematic industry more than by the public. I became friends with a Hollywood TV animator in the early 1970s, Wendell Washer, who had bought his own U-matic and was recording a collection of one episode of every TV cartoon. Then, during Christmas 1975, the first "buy for your own home" Japanese VCRs were advertised to the public, in three incompatible formats: JVC's VHS, Sony's Betamax, and Sanyo's V-Cord. A mutual friend of Washer and myself, Mark Merlino, who is an enthusiastic technophile, immediately bought one. (Unfortunately, he picked the V-Cord, the first of the three to be quickly discontinued.)

Merlino and I were both members of Los Angeles' weekly s-f fan club, the Los Angeles Science Fantasy Society. Merlino started to record s-f programs off TV and bring them on his V-Cord to LASFS meetings and s-f parties. Some of his most popular programs were the Japanese giant-robot half-hour TV cartoons, which fortuitously had just begun on L.A.'s Japanese community TV channel in February 1976. After a few months (this was also during the peak popularity of Marvel Comics' superheroes), a small subgroup developed within the LASFS who encouraged Merlino to emphasize the giant-robot cartoons and forget the other stuff. It was my suggestion to turn the irregular giant-robot cartoon screenings into a separate club with regular, publicized meetings. That club, the Cartoon/Fantasy Organization, first met in May 1977 with Merlino providing the programming on his V-Cord and myself as the secretary, bulletin publisher, and everything else. Cartoon fans in other metropolises like New York and San Francisco started clubs to record Japanese cartoons off their Japanese-community TV channels. So the creation of anime fandom in the U.S. and Canada can be traced directly to the VCR.

The 1980s were the decade of the war for supremacy between Japan Victor Corporation's Video Home System (VHS) and Sony's Betamax formats. Everyone agreed that the Betamax was slightly superior, but the VHS slowly won out because its cassettes could record 120 minutes, allowing families to record complete movies off TV, while the Betamax cassettes only recorded 60 minutes, too short for the average 60$^+$-minute feature film. It seems incredible today, considering the flood of Disney releases to video, but Disney was originally a leader with Universal Studios in the battle to have VCRs and the home copying off

TV declared illegal. (*Sony Corp. of America vs. Universal City Studios*, 1976.) The case was argued up to the U.S. Supreme Court, which ruled in 1984 in favor of Sony and the Betamax. Disney, which had already entered the video market in 1980 for rental cassettes and non-copyable video discs, promptly started selling the *Walt Disney Cartoon Classics* videos. Remember the steadily-diminishing list of "Disney classic features that will never be released on home video"? Today, every Disney film, animated or live-action, is available on VCRs or their successor DVDs. (Except for *Song of the South*, of course.)

Anime fans had long become accustomed to Japanese cartoons made especially for video release. They were called OAVs or OVAs, for original animation videos or original video animation. (The Japanese are great at coining their own English-language abbreviations.) Fans clamored for the American animation studios to begin making OAVs, since they were so successful in Japan. They finally got the first with Warner Home Video's *Tiny Toon Adventures: How I Spent My Vacation* in March 1992, except that WB did not call it an OAV. It was a direct-to-video release. The OAV/OVA abbreviation has never caught on in America, but there are too many direct-to-video animation productions to list. *The Land Before Time XIII: The Wisdom of Friends*, anybody?

Streamline Pictures, the anime licensor where I worked from 1991 to 2002, got caught up in anime fandom's dubbing-vs-subbing video wars. Which was better, an anime dubbed into English, or one in the original Japanese language with subtitles in English? Most American anime licensors promoted the purity of the original sound track, sub-titled, which not incidentally was a lot cheaper to produce than a fully dubbed audio track. Carl Macek at Streamline Pictures was the only producer who insisted on dubbing everything. He got death threats from Japanese-language purists, but he insisted that he made anime videos for the general public rather than for the elite fans; and sales proved that the public would rather listen to an English-language sound track than read subtitles. The wars continued until the DVD replaced the video cassette in 1995 and it became possible to include both an English dubbed sound track and the original Japanese with English subtitles on the same DVD.

Today, multilingual animation DVDs are common. I recently watched an Indian DVD of the Yash Raj Films-Disney release animated feature *Roadside Romeo* in Hindi with subtitles in English and in Malayalam available. It seems like all American animation is available now on DVD, although it isn't, quite. New releases of "lost" and "forgotten" animation are still being announced. Walter Lantz was right: the VCR and its DVD successor have been godsends that have saved the animation industry.

Anime Fandom in North America

Anime fandom in the U.S. and Canada began when the Japanese animated TV program *Raideen* (*Yûsha Raideen; Brave Raideen*) began to be broadcast on American Japanese-community channels, in February 1976.

There were earlier anime TV cartoons on Japanese-community channels—for example, *Ikkyu-san* and *Chobin*—but they "didn't count", for two reasons. Firstly, they were not exciting science-fictional superhero cartoons. *Ikkyu-san* was about a young Buddhist acolyte, the equivalent of a Christian altar boy, solving social problems by non-violent means. *Chobin* (*Hoshi no Ko Chobin; Chobin, the Star Child*) was about a young alien prince (he looked like a short stalk of celery) who came to Earth near a forest, and made friends with Rori, a young human girl, and several talking forest animals. All the others were for little children. *Raideen* and the giant-robot TV cartoons that followed it were a fresh (to Americans) variation on the comic-book costumed superhero formula. This was right at the time that the Marvel superhero comic books were gaining tremendous popularity with American adolescent boys, and DC comics jumped on the bandwagon with the Flash, Green Lantern, the Justice League of America, and others; but American animated cartoons were becoming increasingly censored and non-violent, "for little children". The Japanese s-f animation showed that somebody could still make animated cartoons that teenagers and young adults would be interested in watching.

Secondly, they were before the Christmas 1975 introduction of the home video cassette recorder. It would not have mattered if Japanese TV cartoons were thrilling or boring if they were only available on the obscure Japanese-community channel—usually one per city—in the evenings. By making it possible to record programs and re-show them to like-minded fans, to trade the cartoons shown in one city for those from another city, and to trade recordings of American TV with fans in Japan for their programming (un-subtitled), the VCR made anime fandom possible.

Here are some of the Japanese TV animation shown at early anime club meetings for the first five years, from 1977 to late 1981 or early 1982. This is a chaotic list. Speaking for Los Angeles alone, I was in charge of the anime club bulletin and correspondence. Mark Merlino was in charge of providing the video programming, and I never knew from where he got all of his anime videos. Some were recorded from Los Angeles TV; some were traded with fans in other cities for the anime on their local stations. Some were traded with fans in Japan who wanted American s-f TV programs like *Star Trek*. Some were traded with American fans who got them from rental videos in their local Japanese communities. Some were favorites with dozens of episodes available, while others were samples with only one or two available. The order in which anime programs were shown bore no resemblance to their original broadcast order. Sometimes we would get a program when it was brand-new; at other times we would get a recording made from a Japanese TV rerun that was years old.

Here, then, is what we watched in the early days of anime fandom:

Yûsha Raideen (*Brave Raideen*). This seemed very imaginative to us, but after a few more giant-robot cartoons, we realized that it was just a Japanese stereotypical formula that we were not familiar with in America yet. The scientist father of the teenaged hero is killed by evil space aliens (invariably shown with a demon's horns; "foreign devils") who plan to conquer Earth. The father had just invented, or found in the ruins of a prehistoric civilization, a mighty giant robot warrior that only the hero could "fade into" and pilot. Later, two or three school chums, including The Girl, would get their own craft to become his military squad. *Raideen*'s theme song sounded like a peppy college football fight song.

UFO Senshi Dai Apolon (*UFO Warrior Great Apollo*). Even more high-school football oriented. Takeshi's three pals magically change into their super-football uniforms, and their mini-flying saucers appear when they chant U!, F!, and O! together.

Getta Robo G. (*CombinoRobot G*). The Japanese word "get", or "gat", meant "to combine", so many of the anime s-f series that involved three or five vehicles combining to make one awesome giant vehicle had a "get" or "gat" in the title. *Getta Robo G* was really the sequel to *Getta Robo*, but we did not see the original program until later. Three buddies' individual superscientific vehicles, for Air, Sea, and Land, combined into the huge, all-purpose Getta Robo G. According to widely-believed rumor, the Japanese sponsoring toy companies would go to the engineering colleges and commission students, or hold a contest, to design the most complex giant robot toy that would not fall over on its face, then take the design to an animation studio and commission a TV cartoon around it.

Dr. Saotome, leading the fight to save Earth from the Hundred Demon Empire, builds the ComboDragon (air), ComboLiger (sea), and ComboPoseidon (land) for his three teenage pilots. After being nearly defeated individually during the first half of the program, they combine into the massive Getta Robo G and defeat the demon warrior of the week in the last half. One of the most hissable demons was named either General Hitler or General Hydra, who looked like a tall Adolf

Hitler with a longhorn steer's horns. In Japanese, "Hitler" and "hydra" sound almost the same, and the series' scriptwriters took full advantage of the similarity.

We called this genre the "giant robot programs". I don't remember whether the C/FO invented that term, but we thought that we were just translating a popular Japanese term. By the time that we found out that the Japanese called them "super robots"—and later divided them into super robots and "real" robots—it was too late to change. They were "giant robots" in America, and they stayed giant robots.

Candy Candy. We didn't watch only the boys' adventure anime. We at least sampled the girls' anime. Actually, I was the big rooter for *Candy Candy*, because I was fascinated in this Japanese take on American history. Candy White is a blonde orphan, about ten years old, who becomes a young maid at the estate of a Robber Baron just before World War I. You can tell that the Reagans are Robber Barons because they have a huge mansion near Chicago, dozens and dozens of liveried servants, and regularly go fox hunting in full regalia. Candy has a harsh life as a maid, but she is afraid to displease the head maid who warns her that if her work is not good enough, she will be EXILED TO MEXICO! Cut to a caricature of a Mexican slavemaster who makes the Frito Bandito look like Ricardo Montalban. Candy suffers as she grows up through over two years' worth of half-hour episodes, finally marrying her True Love. *Candy Candy* was even more popular in Italy than in Japan. When Yumiko Igarashi, the *Candy Candy* manga artist upon whose work the TV anime was based, came to the 1980 San Diego Comic-Con, she told Wendy Pini that she was furious at Toei Animation for giving Candy a cute pet albino raccoon, Clint, just for merchandising plush doll purposes. Clint was NOT in the manga!

Jetter Mars. Most early anime fans were already fans of *Astro Boy*. When promotional articles on *Jetter Mars* (or *Jet Mars*; it was translated both ways) showed up in the monthly anime magazines during most of 1977, with the little-boy robot looking so much like Astro Boy, the publicity artwork captured our attention. So when Dr. Tezuka (he liked to be addressed as Dr. Tezuka, even though he never used his medical degree) visited the Cartoon/Fantasy Organization in March 1978, we made sure to ask him about it. Tezuka told us that Toei Animation had commissioned him to create "as close a copy of Mighty Atom (Astro Boy's Japanese name) as he was comfortable with." He did not see much point in just making a duplicate of Mighty Atom with cosmetic differences, so he came up with a little-boy robot who was created by two scientists, Dr.

Kawashimo who gave him artificial intelligence, and Dr. Yamanoue who built his body with superscientific weaponry in it; but no programming to be either good or bad. Dr. Kawashimo wanted to use Jetter Mars to help humanity, while Dr. Yamanoue wanted to use him as a mercenary for the highest bidder. Jetter Mars was mostly a bewildered little robot whose two creators were always arguing that he should follow me; no, not him, me!; no, ME. Tezuka's concept was that Jetter Mars would sometimes follow Dr. Kawashimo and sometimes Dr. Yamanoue, although when he took Dr. Yamanoue's orders, the story would work out that his more violent actions would inadvertently work out for the best for humanity.

Tezuka's contract with Toei was that he would create the basic concept for the series, and the plot outlines for the first five episodes. In episode #6, Dr. Yamanoue was killed off, Jetter Mars went to live permanently with Dr. Kawashimo, and the series became an insipid copy of *Mighty Atom* with kindly Dr. Kawashimo as kindly Dr. Ochanomizu. The C/FO got enough episodes to agree with Tezuka; after episode #5, it went downhill fast. The most memorable thing about the series was that Toei got a real little boy about 7 or 8 years old who did not have any voice acting experience to play Jetter Mars, including singing the lively theme song enthusiastically but very off-key.

***Lupin III**. A rare non-giant-robot favorite was *Lupin III*, a crime-caper-comedy from Tokyo Movie Shinsa based upon a manga by Monkey Punch. Monkey Punch was Kazuhito Kato, the first Japanese professional cartoonist after Osamu Tezuka to become friendly with American fans. Although a pro, he broke all the rules, one of which is that a professional cartoonist should keep an aloof distance from his fans. (Tezuka was a *sensei*; Monkey Punch was a pal.) Kato said that he was born in a tiny seacoast fishing village where his father was a fisherman, his grandfather was a fisherman, his great-grandfather was a fisherman, and he hated fish! He ran away to Tokyo to escape becoming a fisherman, taught himself to draw by studying Sergio Aragones' marginal cartoons in *Mad*, and decided to create a manga around the modern adventures of the grandson of Arsene Lupin, the fictional French gentleman jewel thief by Maurice Leblanc (1864–1941). The manga was a success and Tokyo Movie Shinsha licensed it for animation. Kato often did the opposite of what he was told to do, so when he was told that he couldn't go to the famous San Diego Comic-Con because he didn't speak any English, he started attending right away. He heard about this tiny group of crazy Americans who were nuts for Japanese anime even though they didn't understand any Japanese, decided that we were his kind of people, and looked us up. Naturally, we had to see what he did (or the TV animated version of it).

Lupin III featured the "good guy" world's greatest thief, the grandson of the famous fictional thief who was extremely popular in Japan. (How a French thief had a Japanese grandson was never explained. Kato assumed that by making him an original grandson of a character by a French author who was long dead, he would avoid any rights problems. He was wrong, wrong, wrong!—but that's another story.) Lupin III had four regular associates:

- *Daisuke Jigen*, a wannabe-Chicago gangster who was a never-miss shooter.

- *Ishikawa Goemon XIII*, or "Samurai" in English-language productions, was another ripoff, the supposed descendant of Ishikawa Goemon (1558?-1594), a legendary Robin Hood-like thief who stole from the rich and gave to the poor. The real Goemon was a ninja, not a samurai, but those stupid Americans could never tell the difference.

- *Fujiko Mine* was the femme fatale of the series, a seductive thief who was often Lupin's rival but sometimes his partner. Her trademark was the bubbleheaded sexpot stereotype ("Fujiko Mine" meant roughly "Twin Peaks", a lewd allusion to her prominent breasts), but she was usually smarter than Lupin himself.

- *Inspector Koichi Zenigata*, the final associate, was the policeman who pursued Lupin in every episode. When Lupin started leaving Japan to commit robberies around the world, Zenigata was promoted from a Japanese policeman to an Interpol agent to have jurisdiction to go after Lupin anywhere.

Lupin III had a convoluted animated history. It was first a 23-episode TV series from October 1971 to March 1972. This was before our time, but it was prestigious; Hayao Miyazaki and Isao Takahata directed some of the individual episodes. These were most easily distinguished by Lupin's wearing a green jacket. After five years, a new and much more popular *Lupin III* series was made, running for 155 episodes from October 1977 to October 1980. These "red jacket" episodes were what the early anime fans saw. The first two *Lupin III* theatrical movies were from this period, and Monkey Punch himself gave the C/FO the English-dubbed video of the 1978 first movie. *Lupin III* went on to have a third "pink jacket" TV series (50 episodes, March 1984–December 1985) and lots more theatrical features, but those were well after the first days of anime fandom. The fans at the end of the 1970s loved the sophisticated, adult plots, the snappy dialogue, and Yuji Ono's jazz score.

Anime Fandom in North America, Part 2

Then, in 1978 or 1979, the giant robots began to be replaced by interstellar science-fiction adventure. *Space Cruiser Yamato. Space Pirate Captain Harlock. Galaxy Express 999.* With these and plenty of giant-robot episodes still to be shown at our monthly meetings, we were in Heaven.

Uchu Senkan Yamato (*Space Cruiser Yamato*). By this time, we had begun shopping for manga and the few, rare, anime-related toys in L.A.'s Little Tokyo. The Japanese salesclerks told us that the title translated as *Space Battleship* (not *Cruiser*) *Yamato*. The IJN *Yamato* really had existed, sunk at the end of World War II, and was the biggest battleship ever built by any country! This was the first anime that sent some American fans scrambling to find out more about actual Japanese history. I think that the second thing was to find out the difference between samurai and ninja.

(To digress, the average American of 2014 does not realize how ignorant of Japan the average American of 1977–78 was. Only military historians knew that the real IJN *Yamato* had been the pride of the Imperial Japanese Navy during World War II. Only students of Japanese history—and they were very few in the 1970s—were familiar with the distinction between samurai and ninja. We were vaguely aware that medieval Japan had been ruled by a shogun rather than an emperor, but we didn't understand the difference or know when the shoguns had been replaced by the emperors. Almost no American high schools or even colleges offered courses in the Japanese language. Common Japanese words like bento, chibi, cosplay, and kawaii were unknown in comparison with common French or Spanish words; or Japanese expressions like "yatta", "yosh", and "uso!". It seems incredible today how rapidly the Japanese "cosplay" has replaced the older American English "costuming" or "masquerading". We pioneering anime fans really had to pull ourselves up by our bootstraps.)

There had been a *Space Cruiser Yamato* theatrical movie in Europe in 1977–78, edited from highlights of the 26 TV episodes, and shown in America in an extremely limited release and twice on Channel 5 in Los Angeles during 1978 (first on February 26, and again on October 10). As I recall, the February broadcast was before we had seen any of the individual TV episodes, but Mark Merlino video-recorded it and we watched it at the C/FO several times during 1978. We were hooked by the dramatic plot (in 2199 A.D., Earth was losing a space war, and all life on Earth would die from radioactivity in one year, unless the World War II battleship *Yamato*, rebuilt into a spaceship, could get to the planet Iskandar for the "Cosmo-DNX" and back in time), the eye-catching Earth

Defense Force uniforms, the unusually charismatic villain Desslar/ Desslok, and the awesome score by Hiroshi Miyagawa. (*Uchu Senkan Yamato* was playing in Japan when *Star Wars* was released, and the Japanese quickly imitated the symphonic scoring of *Star Wars'* music by John Williams with a similar symphonic arrangement of *Yamato*'s music by Miyagawa on an LP record.)

The 1978 movie is on YouTube today, so you can see what turned us on. But the movie was so choppy that it increased our eagerness to see the entire TV series. By the October broadcast we had begun to get the 26 separate episodes, with the Japanese thundering opening theme song sung by baritone Isao Sasaki. By the time that all of the Japanese episodes, subtitled, were shown on the Japanese-community channels, the Americanized *Star Blazers* version had begun to be broadcast in September 1979. It was changed so much (the *Yamato* became the *Argo*) that this became the first anime TV series that the early anime fans taunted their American-TV-watching friends with by showing them the uncut Japanese episodes. (*Battle of the Planets* was on American TV by that time, but the Japanese *Gatchaman* was already ancient history on Japanese TV; we did not get video copies until it was rerun on Japanese TV around 1980.)

Uchu Kaizoku Captain Harlock (*Space Pirate Captain Harlock*). Unlike *Uchu Senkan Yamato*, this title was translated literally. It was our second taste of anime space opera, also based on a manga by Reiji Matsumoto. Or Leiji Matsumoto. Or Reiji... (We learned years later that Matsumoto was deliberately jerking the Americans around by alternating the spelling of his first name back and forth. Both are correct.) The first thing that impressed us was the design of the *Arcadia*, Captain Harlock's spaceship. A spaceship with an old-fashioned Spanish galleon's sterncastle, in outer space!? With the Jolly Roger fluttering...in outer space!? Never mind; just shut up and enjoy the melodrama, which was enhanced tremendously by the operatic-quality music by Seiji Yokoyama and the Tokyo Philharmonic Orchestra.

In 2977 A.D. (the 42-episode TV anime was produced starting in 1977, and shown 1978–79), Earth has an interplanetary civilization, but it is falling apart in complacency and laziness. The mysterious space pirate Harlock is trying to shock the public and government back into life by destroying shipments of luxury items, vices like alcohol and drugs, etc. Suddenly, it turns out that Earth is being secretly invaded by an alien race, the plantlike Mazones, who look like beautiful women. Their deadly sabotage is blamed on Harlock, who finds everyone turned against him. Nevertheless, he is the only one strong enough to fight the Mazone and their queen, Rafflesia.

Shortly after Osamu Tezuka's visit to the C/FO in March 1978, we were contacted by Teruko (Pico) Hozumi, the new Hollywood representative of Toei Doga. She asked the tiny club of anime fans to help make the American public and the movie/TV industry anime-conscious. Naturally, we were enthusiastic volunteers. Our first project was to make a big impression at the San Diego Comic-Con that July. Toei provided 16mm prints of the full range of its half-hour TV episodes, which Mark Merlino ran in an unofficial anime video room, and lots of *Captain Harlock* and *Candy Candy* merchandise (model kits, toys, anime books, dolls, etc.) which I offered for sale at a dealer's table, to see whether American comic-book fans would be interested in comics-related materials from TV series that were unknown in the U.S. The girls' merchandise went untouched (in 1978 the Comic-Con had an almost-exclusively male attendance), but the *Captain Harlock* merchandise almost sold out, especially the *Arcadia* items.

The 42 TV episodes are still being followed up by TV and theatrical sequels. A big-budget CGI theatrical feature is due from Toei (which makes and distributes theatrical features as well as producing TV anime) in fall 2014. It opened in Japan on September 7, 2013, at #2 at the Japanese box office, with a weekend gross in U.S. dollars of $1,351,728, but it quickly fell to 9th place, and was out of the Top Ten by its fourth week.

Ginga Teusudo Three-Nine (*Galaxy Express 999*). Another Matsumoto winner, this show appeared on Japanese-community TV while *Space Pirate Captain Harlock* was still running. If Harlock's deep-space pirate ship looked impractical, what were we to make of an interstellar railroad train—with a steam engine, yet—that toured the Milky Way galaxy, traveled to the Andromeda galaxy, and only stopped at Earth once a year!? But *Galaxy Express 999* was awesomely exotic (opening theme sung by Isao Sasaki again) and we loved it. So did the Japanese; it ran for 113 TV episodes (1978 to 1981), two theatrical features, two TV specials, and three multi-episode OAV (original animation video) sequels.

In the far future when humanity has filled the galaxy, mankind is divided into human commoners and an elite aristocracy who can afford to have their brains transferred into incredibly expensive immortal robot bodies. Tetsuro, a poor 12-year-old human boy (anime fans complained that his character design was unrealistically ugly; Matsumoto replied that it was a self-portrait), is urged by his dying mother to somehow get one of the robot bodies, which are rumored to be available free in Andromeda. While he is at the galactic terminal, Tetsuro is offered free passage on the 999 if he will agree to become the traveling companion of a mysterious Russian-costumed woman who looks just like his mother. (Her Japanese name could be written in English as either Maeter, which is Latin for mother, or Maetel. The translators chose Maetel, to make it a unique name.) In each episode, the 999 stops at a different planet, and Tetsuro has an adventure which becomes a learning experience.

Captain Future. This was Toei Doga's "authorized imitation of *Star Wars*". The Toei executives reportedly said, "George Lucas says that *Star Wars* is his homage to all the space opera magazines and movies that he saw in his youth. Let's find out what some of those magazines were and license them." The *Captain Future* pulp magazine ran for 17 issues from 1940–44; most of its stories were written by s-f author Edmond Hamilton. The publisher told him to make the series a futuristic imitation of the popular *Doc Savage*, so Hamilton created the incredibly handsome and brave spaceman Curtis Newton and his three comedy-relief, always-arguing but loyal assistants, Grag the robot, Otho the android, and Simon Wright, the disembodied brain of his father's partner floating in a customized jar. They had adventures opposing evil space emperors and similar villains. For the TV anime, Toei added a romantic interest and a hero-worshipping tagalong kid, Ken Scott. I had read the old pulp magazine (great fun; you can't tell me that Hamilton didn't have his tongue in cheek when he wrote them), and we expected to be great fans of the 53-episode 1978–79 series, but the quality dropped off so sharply after the pilot episode that we quickly gave up on it.

Besides giant robots, space opera, and *Lupin III*, early anime fandom sampled other TV anime, but either because it wasn't to our taste or because we could not get more than a few episodes, we did not watch other series regularly. Matsumoto had others that were only so-so, such as *Planet Robot Danguard Ace* (the humongous giant robot Danguard Ace protecting humanity from the tyrannical Chancellor Doppler of the planet Promete) and *SF Saiyuki Starzinger* (*The Journey to the West/ Monkey King* legend retold as space opera, with three cyborg/alien bodyguards escorting the Princess of the Moon across the galaxy). Some that we followed for a half-dozen or so episodes included:

Gattiger, or *Cho Supercar Gattiger*, which is somewhat redundant since it means *Super Supercar Gattiger*, ran for 25 episodes, from 1977–78 from Wako Productions, and was it wacky! It combined the giant-robot formula with racing cars. We never got the first episode, so we didn't know whether a reason was ever given, but somehow the fate of the world depended on a round-the-world auto race between humanity's team (consisting of the stereotypical teenage hero who is the Gattiger's inventor's son, his girl friend, his beefy best friend, and the little kid) and the Demon Empire's, or Black Demon Empire's, team, who were of course demons. The winner got control of the earth, and naturally the demons cheated like crazy. Oh, did I mention that the teenage hero's mysterious mother is the Demon Empire's princess? The human team's racecars, which were also invented by the hero's father, could go about 450 miles an hour, and at the crisis point in each episode could link together at top speed into the Supercar Gattiger. If you were driving across rocky terrain or along a twisty mountain road at 450 miles an hour, would you care to get close enough to another car to lock onto it? Anime fans either liked *Gattiger* for giggles or hated it for silliness, although we appreciated that it was done as absolutely straight-faced melodrama.

Hana no Ko Lun Lun (*Lun Lun the Flower Child*) was Toei Doga's magical little girl fantasy of 1979–80. Toei or some other anime studio produced one of these every year from...well, the first ever was *Sally the Witch* in 1966 (created by Mitsuteru Yokoyama, the creator of *Gigantor*, who acknowleged the American TV series *Bewitched* as his inspiration), and the most recent that I know of is *Magical Girl Madoka of the Magus* (*Puella Magi Madoka Magica*), January-April 2011, interrupted by the Tohoku earthquake and tsunami, with a theatrical movie released on October 26, 2013. I would be surprised if there has ever been a time between *Sally the Witch* and *Magical Girl Madoka* when there was not a magical little girl anime on TV.

Lun Lun Flower, a sweet little Swiss teenager, is persuaded by Nouveau, a talking St. Bernard, and Gateaux, a fluffy white cat, to join them in searching all over Europe for a magic flower that will reveal the missing princess of the Flower Planet. Surprise! she turns out to be Lun Lun, although at the climax she renounces her throne to return to Earth and her adoptive parents, whom she loves, and the boy whom she wants to marry. This series was mildly interesting because the writers took every advantage to work in the almost-forgotten Victorian-era "language of flowers"—the amaryllis means pride, the lavender means devotion, the magnolia means love of nature, mint means suspicion, the pear blossom means lasting friendship but not love, etc.

Seton Dobutsuki Risu no Bana (*Banner, the Gray Squirrel*). This was supposedly a 26-episode 1979 anime adaptation of Ernest Thompson Seton's 1922 children's book *Bannertail: The Story of a Gray Squirrel*. Seton died in 1946 and the book was forgotten in America by the 1970s. I can't imagine why Nippon Animation decided to animate it, but the studio did a two-part series of adaptations of Seton's forest-animal novels, *Bannertail* and the 1919 *Monarch: The Big Bear of Tallac* (as *Jackie, the Bear Cub*). I had not read Seton's novel (I have since), but I knew that he was the author of "true-life" animal books for children, like Felix Salten with *Bambi* and *Perri* in Europe, so I strongly doubted that his woodland animals wore clothing and quoted Shakespeare as Nippon Animation showed them. The C/FO locked onto *Banner* by accident; we just happened to pick as a sample episode—#13, "Lure of the Mushrooms"—in which Banner accidentally eats a hallucinogenic mushroom and freaks out! (Yes, it is in Seton's novel; apparently it is a common danger for Eastern U.S. gray squirrels.) The other episodes were not nearly as interesting and we soon gave it up as too infantile for us. (I personally objected to the owl's flying with a pigeon's noisy flutter; owls are silent flyers.)

In retrospect, it's surprising that during the first five years of anime fandom, 1976–1981, the Los Angeles club got almost no episodes of the original *Getter Robo* or *Gatchaman* or *UFO Robot Grandizer*, and we only managed to trade videos for a handful of episodes of *Cyborg 009*—it was shown on NYC's Japanese-community channel but not in Los Angeles. The availability of anime in America during the late 1970s and early 1980s was very much a hit-or-miss affair.

In 1982, two genres brand-new in anime reached us, and the earliest days of anime fandom were over: teenagers from outer space, and more realistic mobile-suit battle armor replacing the giant robots. Anime fandom would never be the same!

The "Teenagers from Outer Space" Genre

The Teenagers from Outer Space genre consists almost entirely of a single program, *Urusei Yatsura*. It was so massively popular and influential that it practically fills the 1980s all by itself.

Urusei Yatsura began as a weekly manga by Rumiko Takahashi in 1978. The tankobon paperback collections began in 1980. The TV animation began on October 14, 1981; I am guessing that the C/FO did not start getting video copies until early 1982. Those were "raw" copies from Japanese TV, untranslated. We had to guess what was going on, but it was clear enough from the visuals alone, and it was hysterically funny. By the time that new *Urusei Yatsura* animation was finished in 1991, there were either 195 or 219 TV episodes (the first season consisted of two fifteen-minute stories per half-hour episode, so the discrepancy depends upon whether those are considered as one or two episodes), six theatrical features, and nine OAV (original animation videos). And tons of merchandising. Takahashi, who had begun as a shy early-20s cartoonist, ended as the richest woman in Japan from all the royalties pouring in. (By the time the *Urusei Yatsura* animation ended, Takahashi had already gone on to *Maison Ikkoku, Ranma ½,* and other creations, all of which brought additional floods of royalties.)

The plot follows (usually comically) Ataru Moroboshi, an oversexed Japanese high-school student; Lum, a cute space invader; and their friends, families, and acquaintances. Initially, Earth is confronted by a massive flying saucer, the forerunner of an invincible fleet. They have come to add Earth to their space empire—but their laws say that if their champion can be defeated by the invaded world's champion in one week, they will go away peacefully. Their super-computer has picked Ataru as Earth's champion, and Lum, the leading invader's teenaged daughter, is their champion. (Typical Japanese nepotism.) Ataru wins by a blatantly male chauvinist pig ruse, but Lum misinterprets his victory as a proposal of marriage. She insists on staying on Earth, moving into the Moroboshi household as Ataru's fiancée, and enrolling in Tomobiki High School as a fellow student.

One of the reasons that *Urusei Yatsura* remained so popular was that it was constantly growing and expanding. Ataru's classmates and teachers were slowly added. Lum's teenaged space friends joined her on Earth, one by one. When Lum first moved in with the Moroboshis, Ataru's mother cowered before her. By the time a year had passed, she was treating Lum like a daughter. In one episode around 1982 or '83, when a neighbor cowers as Mrs. Moroboshi used to do, she does a double-take and says to herself, "It's true! You really do get used to anything."

Urusei Yatsura also wittily equated the space invaders with familiar Japanese mythological characters. Lum's family and the main space invader army were traditional oni demons with horns and fangs. Lum had cute little horns, but her father was not something you wanted to encounter alone at night. Lum's space friends were thinly-disguised Japanese goddesses and supernatural beings, such as Princess Oyuki of Neptune = an icy snow maiden; Ran = a hone-onna, a beautiful succubus; Benten = Benzaiten, the Shinto goddess who protects Japan; etc. Many episodes sent the American fans to books on Japanese history, mythology, or culture to find out who a new character was a pastiche of, or to the language books to find out what a visual pun meant. Other in-group jokes were that "Ataru Moroboshi" literally means "to be struck by a falling star", indicating the character's constant bad luck. In the contest in the first episode, the number 4 on Ataru's sports shirt is the Japanese equivalent of 13, the bad-luck number.

Ever since *Uchu Senkan Yamato*, we tried to translate the titles of each new series to be aware of what we were really watching. *Urusei Yatsura* was the first title that really flummoxed us. We ended up translating it as *Those Obnoxious Aliens* or *Those Annoying Aliens*, but we were aware that neither translation did justice to the really horrible Japanese slang/pun. There is a Japanese phrase, "urusai yatsura", meaning "obnoxious people", but "UruSEI" means "the planet/star Uru". "Urusei" alone means "Shut up!", usually shouted. "Yatsura" is derogatory slang meaning bums, jerks, no-goods, worthless people, etc., so "urusei yatsura" roughly means "those worthless jerks from the planet Uru". When we were asked what the title really meant, we translated it loosely as "those lousy aliens from the planet Uru have moved into our neighborhood, and the property values have gone to Hell". Significantly, in retrospect, the mild arguing over whether "Urusei Yatsura" should be translated as "Those Annoying Aliens" or as "Those Obnoxious Aliens" was indicative of the later serious feuding within the C/FO that wrecked the club.

Urusei Yatsura was For Us. Previous Japanese TV cartoons were subsidized by their sponsors through toy sales, which usually meant the parents buying the toys for their children. *Urusei Yatsura*'s fans were teenagers and young adults who bought their own merchandise: manga volumes, video games, videos (a tiny percentage of sales; videos were really expensive in Japan), and above all, records! The TV animation was produced by Kitty Films (actually subcontracted to Studio Pierrot), a subsidiary of Kitty Records, which was itself a subsidiary of the Kitty Music Corporation. Instead of pushing toys, *Urusei Yatsura* was aimed at pushing pop songs that the teen market would hopefully buy as records. While other TV anime programs started with one opening credits sequence and theme song and stuck with it through the end, *Urusei Yatsura* changed its opening every season to introduce and promote a new theme song, available on a single at record shops throughout Japan. The theatrical features had room for several songs.

Other examples of Teenagers from Outer Space during the '80s were surprisingly from America.

Galaxy High School ran for 13 episodes, from September 13, 1986, to December 6, 1986, on CBS. The Japanese animation studio Tokyo Movie Shinsha (today TMS Entertainment) had opened an office in Los Angeles and was aggressively trying to break into Hollywood's 1980s TV cartoon market. It had already produced the 1984 *Mighty Orbots*. TMS was aware of the popularity of *Urusei Yatsura* with Japanese teens, and pitched a similar series for American TV. Technically, *Galaxy High* was a reversal of the plot: two human high school students amidst alien teens at an interstellar high school. CBS bought the basic concept and assigned Chris Columbus to develop it and write the first episode.

Two American teenagers, Doyle Cleverlobe and Aimee Brightower, are selected to attend Galaxy High School on the asteroid Flutor. In their American high school, Doyle is a hotshot sports star while Aimee is a brainy wallflower, but at Galaxy High, Doyle's conceitedness makes him unpopular while Aimee's friendly attitude makes her very popular. Aimee shows Doyle how to make friends by joining Galaxy High's psych-hockey team as a team player instead of a glory hog. Other galactic students, all comically alien, are the class president, Milo de Venus (instead of no arms, he has too many), Gilda Gossip (mouths on six weaving tentacles over her head), Booey Bubblehead (a girl with a big transparent bubble for a head, so everyone can see how empty it is), and Creep, a shy, yellow, marshmallowlike flying alien with a big crush on Aimee. The teachers and staff of Galaxy High were equally bizarre. Chris Columbus reportedly named Doyle, Booey, and Aimee after his brother and sisters. Despite being very popular, CBS did not renew it. (Probably because it had almost no merchandise.)

Teenagers from Outer Space. This was a role-playing game, published by R. Talsorian Games on February 1, 1987. Mike Pondsmith, a leading developer of new RPG games and the founder of R. Talsorian Games, was a big anime fan. He developed *Mekton*, featuring giant robots and admittedly heavily influenced by *Mobile Suit Gundam*, in 1984. In late 1986 or early 1987, Pondsmith developed *Teenagers from Outer Space*, inspired almost entirely by *Urusei Yatsura*. A second edition in 1989 was a bit more generic, with some influences of *Galaxy High School*. (There was a third edition in 1997.)

For the record, there was a *Teenagers from Outer Space* 1959 black-and-white horror movie that had no influence on any of this. The 1959 movie is a *Mystery Science Theater 3000* favorite, although it was never a very serious horror movie in the first place.

Cat Girls

This is slightly out of order, but it was around the mid-1980s that we began to notice the Japanese obsession with cat girls, and the difference between American animal-people and Japanese animal-people.

Cat girls. The Japanese invented them.

What distinguishes Japanese "cat girls" from Western anthropomorphized/funny animals in general is that they are drawn as humans with only the animal ears and a tail. Western funny animals, including animalized humans, are drawn with full animal heads and fur (or feathers or scales, if they are bird-men or reptile-men). They are basically the animals standing on two legs. The first American anime fans were startled by the Japanese depiction, but quickly accepted it as a traditional Japanese cultural convention.

The first anime "cat girl" was actually a whole cartoon of "fox people". In November 1949, director Mitsuya Seo, famous for directing the wartime propaganda animated films *Momotaro's Sea Eagles* (March 1943) and *Momotaro's Divine Sea Warriors* (March 1945), made the 33-minute *The King's Tail* (*Osama no Shippo*) for Nihon Doga, a.k.a. Nihon Manga Eigasha (Japan Cartoon Film Studio). It was a variation of the tale of the emperor's new clothes, about a tailless fox king in a kingdom of anthropomorphized foxes, but the foxes were drawn as humans with only fox ears and tails.

American fans became aware of cat girls during the 1980s, more from direct-to-video releases (original anime videos, or OAVs) than from theatrical or TV animation. Most of this animation is adapted from earlier manga. Two of the first anime cat girls were AnnaPuma and UniPuma, the mildly raunchy but very spectacular sisters in Masamune Shirow's futuristic comedy **Dominion: Tank Police**. The manga was published in 1985; the first of three anime OAVs came in May 1988. AnnaPuma and UniPuma were originally android love dolls that the villain Buaku enhanced with artificial intelligence to become his henchgirls. After Buaku disappeared, the authorities decided that the cat girls were not responsible for Buaku's programming of them, and tried to rehabilitate them by making them members of the Tank Police, with dubious results.

Another early manga and OAV was Johji Manabe's **Outlanders**; the manga in 1985–87, and the OAV in December 1986. *Outlanders* featured the aliens Princess Kahm and Battia, who looked like cute teenaged girls except that Kahm had a ram's horns and Battia was a cat girl. Kahm deliberately destroyed Earth all by herself.

In **Dragon Half**, a warrior knight eloped with the dragon that he was supposed to slay. The result: their daughter Mink, who looked like a normal teenage girl with miniature dragon's horns, wings growing out of her back, tail, and the ability to breathe fire when she lost her temper. *Dragon Half* was one of the first anime OAVs licensed for release in America, in 1993 by A.D. Vision. The reason is that the license was very cheap; *Dragon Half* was such a failure in Japan that the series was cancelled halfway through, so the American fans never found out how the hilarious story ended.

A stand-out cat girl was Pink, in the erotic (we don't say porno) 1994–95 OAV series **Dragon Pink**. This was a parody of role-playing games, with the busty but innocent cat girl-slave dragged along on quests by the warrior Santa. Others with Santa included Bobo, an axe-wielding barbarian, and the elf mage Pierce. The adventures usually involved Pink getting captured, stripped nude, bound and molested, while the questers arrived too late to rescue her.

Ruin Explorer was a 1995 four-video OAV series, a humorous parody of fantasy treasure-seeking stereotypes. In a world consisting of nothing but crumbling, ruined cities, the young women Fam and Ihrie search for the Ultimate Power (which everyone else in that world is also after). Fam looks like a cat girl but is supposed to be a Wiccan sorceress. Ihrie, the dominant one of the pair, is a tomboyish human girl except that she is cursed to turn into a mouse whenever she tries to use magic herself. After a 1998 American release by A.D. Vision, the new distributor Maiden Japan announced in March 2013 that it had picked up the license, and then in July 2013 re-released it as *Ruin Explorers*. (This is a classic example of Japanese-English language confusion. The original Japanese title is *Ruin Explorer*, in English but singular since the Japanese language does not recognize plurals. The 1998 American release was titled *Ruin Explorers*, since there are two heroines. This was better English, but it caused some anime purists to object to the added 's'.)

The Vision of Escaflowne was a very popular 26-episode TV series in 1996. Most of its cast was human, but it did have the 13-year-old cat girl Merle, who spent most of her time being jealous of the schoolgirl protagonist from Earth, Hitomi. Older cat girls appeared later in the series.

Hyper Police, with 25 episodes aired in 1997, featured a whole Shinjuku police force of—well, the chief was a Shinto god, and the regular cops included Batanen, a werewolf who looked human with a wolf's ears and tail; Tommy, a funny-animal dog; Sakura, a traditional kitsune who looked like a sexy human woman with eight fox tails, going for her ninth; and the main character, Natsuki Sasahara, whose father was human and whose mother was 2/3 cat. (?) Natsuki looked like a 17-year-old human girl with a cat's tail and both human and cat ears.

Outlaw Star was a 26-episode TV space-opera series in 1998, loosely based on Stevenson's *Treasure Island* that was *much* better than Disney's later *Treasure Planet*. The cast was human except for the comic-relief alien cat girl Aisha Clanclan, princess of the Ctarl Ctarl, who is at first a reluctant member of the human group seeking the treasure planet, but comes to enjoy their "familyhood" and embraces their quest for the journey, though not its eventual end.

Night Warriors: Darkstalkers' Revenge was a 4-episode OAV airing in 1997 and based upon the very popular video game that introduced the later *Street Fighter* concept. The supernatural families of Dimitri Maximoff, vampire, and Morrigan Aensland, succubus, are fighting for control of the Demon World. Felicia, a bakeneko or cat-demon, is one of Dimitri's family. As a cat demon, Felicia looks like a cat girl with enhanced feline features: carnivorous teeth, cat paws/mittens, and furry clawed legs up to the thighs. She is the most sympathetic character to humans, wanting to be a pop singer in the human world. She tried to join a touring company of the musical *Cats*, but was rejected because her "costume" was too revealing. She was raised as a child by a Roman Catholic nun, and is confused by human religion but is generally predisposed to Catholicism.

Di Gi Charat appeared in Japan in 1998 as the ultra-cute cat girl mascot in advertising for Broccoli Inc.'s video games. The adverts were so popular that Broccoli quickly spun her off as a manga heroine, and then a 2001 TV anime series. Di Gi Charat, abbreviated Dejiko, and her tagalong friends Petit Charat (Puchiko) and Gema (for gamer), work in the Gamer video game store in Akihabra, Tokyo's electronics district, where the best video game shops are located. The 2001 TV series was so popular that there have been *Di Gi Charat* animated TV sequels, OAVs, a 20-minute theatrical "movie", and of course video games. Gamers has even opened an Anime Gamers shop in Los Angeles, devoted more to Broccoli's anime and manga books and DVDs and related merchandise (girls' school accessories, coin purses, etc.) than to video games. The *Di Gi Charat* DVD cover shows Dejiko (green hair) and Puchiko (brown hair) with cat ears, and Dejiko's rival Rab-en-rose with purple hair and rabbit ears. Another popular Broccoli anime and video game title has been *Galaxy Angel(s)*, a comedic s-f series about the misadventures of a squad of five ditsy all-girl interstellar policewomen, one of whom is Mint Blancmange, a turquoise-haired, lop-eared bunny girl.

Tokyo Mew Mew, with 52 episodes aired in 2002–2003, was a *big* hit with little girls. Five schoolgirls get the DNA of almost-extinct animals and fight alien demons out to destroy Earth's ecology.

Tokyo Mew Mew was Americanized by 4Kids Entertainment as *Mew Mew Power,* and heavily criticized by the fans for all the cuts of any scene showing Japanese ethnicity. There was a manga sequel in Japan, *Tokyo Mew Mew a la Mode.*

For a full discussion, refer to the entry for *Tokyo Mew Mew* in "Magical Little Witches", in chapter 2 of this book.

Phew! That's enough about the cat girls.

The Many Programs of Go Nagai

It was the giant robot TV cartoons on Japanese-community TV channels that introduced Japanese anime to American fandom in 1977. *Yûsha Raideen, UFO Senshi Dai Apolon,* and *Getta Robo G* were the first to come to America (in Los Angeles, anyway). These were so important that they, and the creator of the giant robot genre, Go Nagai, are worth a digression before we leave them.

There seemed to be dozens of giant robot TV programs, and many of them looked too much alike to be attributed to their being all giant robot shows. In the following months, we started to get sample episodes of other Japanese TV cartoons, and many that weren't giant robot programs showed a similarity of art styles. It couldn't be because they were all from the same animation studio, either, because they weren't. But they were all created by the same cartoonist, Go Nagai. We gradually learned that Nagai had not only created the giant robot craze, but almost as many others as there were genres of anime. He started a company, Dynamic Productions, to create manga, anime, and toy designs to order.

Here are some of them.

Mazinger Z

92 episodes | December 3, 1972 – September 1, 1974

Let's start with this because it is the most important, and the first of them all—the program that set off the giant robot craze. *Mazinger Z* aired on Fuji TV on Sundays at 7:00 p.m., and was created by cartoonist Go Nagai's Dynamic Production Co., first for the Bandai toy manufacturer or its Popy subsidiary, and then for Toei Animation after Bandai (or Popy) confirmed that it would sponsor it. In other words, the giant robot toys came first, and the story was written around them.

An international archaeological team discovers the ruins of a lost civilization that had giant robots sixty feet tall. The German member of the team, Dr. Hell, kills all of the other archaeologists except for the Japanese Prof. Kabuto, who escapes. Dr. Hell plans to use the lost technology to create an army of mechanical beasts to conquer the world. Prof. Kabuto intends to build his own army to stop him, but he only builds one prototype, Mazinger Z, before he is killed by Hell's agents. Prof. Kabuto's teenage grandson, Koji, becomes Mazinger Z's pilot to foil Dr. Hell's mechanical-beast-of-the-week.

Koji was joined by his high school pals and his girl friend with their own giant robots, which of course were also available as toys. Most popular with the adolescent boy viewers was Koji's girl friend Sayaka's female giant robot, Aphrodite A, which fired missiles from its chest. "Fire tit missiles!"

Mazinger Z was so popular that "he" was deliberately destroyed in battle prematurely (Koji Kabuto was only critically wounded) so he could be replaced by an improved giant robot, which meant ALL-NEW TOYS. This was *Great Mazinger*, which ran for 56 more episodes, from September 8, 1974, to September 28, 1975. By then, Koji Kabuto was out of the hospital, and it was time for *UFO Robo Grandizer*, which ran for 74 episodes, from October 5, 1975, to February 27, 1977. (The main thing that I remember about *UFO Robot Grandizer* was that it was supposed to be set in the American Wild West, and the Japanese clearly did not know the difference between longhorn steers and dairy cows. Or maybe this was Nagai's sense of humor; with Go-chan, it was hard to tell. A stampede of dairy cows is a unique sight.)

The important fact is that *Mazinger G* was essentially a single TV cartoon series in the guise of a half-hour toy commercial that lasted for 222 episodes and five years. Japan's toy companies took notice in a big way.

Here are samples of a very few of Nagai's other giant robot TV cartoons. (They include *Getter Robo G*, which I discussed in a previous chapter.)

Kotetsu Jeeg
Steel Jeeg
46 episodes | October 5, 1975 - August 29, 1976

Professor Shiba, a famous scientist and archaeologist, was examining the super-scientific relics of the ancient Yamatai Kingdom. When his son, race car driver Hiroshi, was mortally wounded in a laboratory accident, Prof. Shiba used Yamatai science to keep him alive by turning him into a cyborg. Then it turned out that the Yamatai were still around and plotting to conquer Japan. Queen Himika had Prof. Shiba killed, which of course made Hiroshi her mortal enemy. Hiroshi uses his cyborg power to become the head of Jeeg, the giant robot, to fight the Yamatai.

We did not know it at the time, but Nagai used some semi-legendary Japanese history from 200–300 A.D. in the names of the Yamatai and Queen Himika.

Gaiking
Daikuu Maryuu Gaiking; Gaiking, the Demon Dragon of the Heavens
44 episodes | April 1, 1976 - January 27, 1977

The crews of Gaiking, the giant robot, and its semi-transformable support vehicle, The Great Space Dragon, fought to save Earth against the Dark Horror Army from the planet Zeta. The Good Guys were the crew of The Great Space Dragon, which carried a wide range of weapons for Gaiking. Gaiking's pilot was Sanshiro Tsuwabuki, a famous baseball player.

This was the first giant robot series set in different international locales instead of all in Japan. When it was produced, Toei Animation credited a minor Dynamic Prod. staffer as the author in an attempt to avoid paying Nagai higher royalties. Nagai sued, and won after a legal battle that lasted more than ten years.

Govarian

Psycho Armor Govarian
26 episodes | July 6, 1983 - December 28, 1983

In the future, the Garadain Empire is conquering Earth. Zeku Alba, a scientist from an alien planet conquered by the Garadains, escapes to Earth and forms a team of international youths to fight the Garadains. The most talented of the international squad is naturally the Japanese boy, Isamu, whose family was killed by the Garadains. He uses psychogenesis power to activate the giant robot Govarian to fight the Garadains, assisted by two teammates who have giant robots of their own.

This series had a more interstellar and futuristic plot than Nagai usually wrote. He created it for the Knack studio, which has the reputation of one of the poorer in Japan.

God Mazinger

23 episodes | April 15, 1984 - September 30, 1984

Mazinger Z, Great Mazinger, Shin (New) Mazinger, God Mazinger—the name "Mazinger" was solid gold to Japan's TV animation and toy industries, and Nagai took full advantage of it. Teenager Yamato Hino is transported to a parallel world where the evil Empire of Dinosaurs is conquering the good Kingdom of Mu. Mu has a legend that a giant prehistoric stone statue of the god Mazinger will come to life when called by someone named Yamato. Yamato activates the statue and uses it to defeat the Dinosaurians. He remains in the parallel world as the royal champion of Mu. See the medieval European Jewish legend of the Golem for something similar. Tokyo Movie Shinsa/TMS Entertainment produced this one.

Panda-Z—the Robonimation

30 episodes | April 12, 2004 – November 1, 2004

Giant robot pandas!? Never let it be said that Nagai couldn't laugh at himself. This program for little children, mostly in pantomime, was actually created by Shuichi Oshida, with Nagai's approval, and was produced by Bee Media and Synergy Japan.

Pan-Taron, a super-deformed robot panda, is the pilot of the Panda-Z giant robot in Robonimal City. They fight against the Warunimal forces led by the evil Skullpander.

Let's save some room for Nagai's non-giant robot anime series:

Devilman

39 episodes | July 8, 1972 - April 7, 1973

Teenaged Akira Fudo is possessed by the demon Amon. He has enough will power to defeat the demon, and uses its supernatural power to battle other demons which mostly threaten his girlfriend, Miki, and her kid brother, Tare.

Devilman pioneered serious supernatural horror on TV for children. It has been extremely popular to the present, appearing in OAVs, a live-action feature, video games, manga by Nagai, and novels by Nagai's older brother Yasutaka Nagai, with illustrations by Go Nagai, as well as a TV series remake featuring the other gender, *Devilman Lady*.

Dororon Enma-kun

25 episodes | October 4, 1973 – March 28, 1974

Enma-kun means Li'l Enma, and Enma is a Japanese name for the Devil, so Enma-kun is roughly a Japanese version of Harvey Comics' *Hot Stuff*. The series was a *Devilman*-Lite for younger children.

Li'l Enma was the nephew of the King of Hell, about ten years old. Despite his youth, he was made the leader of the Ghost Patrol (nepotism counts), assigned with child snow maiden Yukiko-Hime and Kapaeru, a kappa (a traditional Japanese river demon supposed to drown the unwary), to track down spirits that escape from Hell and return to Earth, and bring them back to Hell. Bloodthirsty Li'l Enma usually killed them instead. (It was never explained how you can kill a ghost.) In the manga and TV series, there is a massive jailbreak of ghosts who escape to the Big City (assumed by Japanese viewers to be Tokyo; by American viewers to be NYC), and the Ghost Patrol is assigned to return them to Hell. Unknown to them, the ghosts have banded together and are plotting to overthrow the King of Hell. Complications ensue. Comedy-relief was provided by Dracula, who had been assigned as the resident demon in charge of the Big City, but who had degenerated into a drunken wino. Enma appoints Dracula as his assistant, but Dracula resents having to take orders from a kid and is always trying to sabotage him.

The original 1973–1974 TV series was a supernatural comedy roughly like Beetlejuice, but a 2011 12-episode remake (produced by an animation studio with the unlikely name of Brains Base), broadcast at 2:10–2:40 a.m., was played for straight adult suspense-horror.

Cutey Honey

25 episodes | October 13, 1973 - March 30, 1974

If *Devilman* introduced supernatural horror to children's TV, *Cutey Honey* introduced SEX to children's TV.

Honey Kisaragi is a 16-year-old student at the Saint Chapel School for Girls, a Catholic school where all the other girls and woman teachers are mildly humorous lesbians. The Earth is secretly invaded by the Panther Claw gang, who are more menacing lesbian monsters. The Panther Claws murder Honey's scientist father to steal his invention that will make them all-powerful. Unknown to anyone, Honey is actually a super android, and her father put his invention in her to bring her to life. So the Panther Claws are after Honey to steal the invention from her (one of the Panthers has a crush on her). Honey learns to control her power to change into other specialized girls, such as Hurricane Honey, a biker; Flash Honey, a news photographer; Fancy Honey, a model; Misty Honey, a rock star; and others, including her "real" form, a pink-haired super sword duelist. Honey is supposedly helped by two boys who are the sons of one of her father's friends, but they spend more time trying to get into her pants, and she spends more time rescuing them from the Panther Claws. When Honey changes into one of her other personas, the change in her costume leaves her nude for a split-second, which made the TV series extremely popular with adolescent boys.

Despite all of the outrageous elements, *Cutey Honey* was popular enough to generate an OAV series, two new animated TV series, a live-action movie, and a live-action TV series.

Kekko Kamen
Masked Kekko

This was *Cutey Honey* carried to an extreme. Mayumi Takahashi is a student at Toenail of Satan's Spartan Institute of Higher Education. The mildly humorous lesbians in *Cutey Honey* are over-the-top vicious burlesques here, along with equal-time exaggerated parodies of homosexual muscle-boys. Mayumi/Kekko protects the other students as a mysterious avenger who wears a mask. Just a mask. Nothing else. This was a manga that everyone assumed could never be filmed. Little did they know.

Kekko Kamen never made it to TV, but there were two animated OAVs in August 1991 and March 1992, and ten live-action movies. YouTube has the OAV credits, but they are censored for American viewers. Incidentally, listen to the American announcer and you will understand why most anime fans originally preferred to watch anime with the original Japanese voices and subtitles, though I will admit that the quality of American anime voice-acting has gotten much better than it was in the early 1990s, when it was believed that the tiny and cash-strapped anime specialty companies relied upon enthusiastic amateur anime fans, who would almost pay you for the privilege of becoming a voice actor, to dub their videos.

Magical Tickle
45 episodes | March 6, 1978 - January 29, 1979

This series proved that Go Nagai could create a standard young girls' magical little witch program when he wanted to. Chiiko, a shy 11-year-old schoolgirl, gets a birthday present of a magical book that, when opened, releases Chikkuru (Tickle), a fairy who was imprisoned for using her powers to play practical jokes. Chikkuru uses her magic to make everyone think that she is Chiiko's twin sister. The two were the first "magical little witch" team, and were obviously inspired by Pink Lady, the two mega-popular pop singers of the moment.

Despite Magical Tickle being a standard children's TV cartoon, it had an unusual origin. It was produced by Toei Co., Ltd., not its Toei Animation studio subsidiary, and its episodes were subcontracted to several other studios. including Nippon Sunrise.

Go Nagai (real name: Kiyoshi Nagai; Go, or "five" in English, is a childhood nickname because he was a fifth son) was born on September 6, 1945. He started as a 15-year-old assistant to Shotaro Ishinomori, and in 1967 published his own first manga, *Harenchi Gakuen (Shameless School)*, full of risqué humor. It was controversial but extremely popular, being adapted into four live-action movies and a 26-episode live-action TV series before any of his animated TV adaptions appeared. (*Shameless School* was finally animated as a 47-minute OAV in 1996.) Go became notorious as the first author/artist of erotic, as distinct from pornographic, manga, and for the virulent protests against his comics and TV animation by the Japanese PTA.

Go founded Dynamic Pro in April 1969 with his brothers to create manga, and ideas and designs for toys and TV cartoons. Nagai or one of Dynamic Pro's staff artists usually produced a manga timed to appear just before the toy or TV animation came out, giving the impression that they were based on the manga rather than the other way around. Dynamic Pro was one of the first Japanese companies to require written contracts instead of just a publisher's or animation studio's verbal promise of royalties.

From 1972 through the end of the 1970s, virtually all of Nagai's original "too hot for TV" manga were adopted into TV cartoons, arguably establishing the brief nude shower scenes that have become standard in

Japanese TV animation. Since the end of the 1970s, Nagai has produced fewer original ideas but a tremendous number of TV and OAV remakes, spinoffs, and sequels to his famous 1970s TV series, including lots of live-action motion pictures.

More Giant Robots!

Don't think that all of the giant robot TV cartoons were created by Go Nagai. He may have invented them, but others quickly jumped onto the, er, giant robots. The giant robots were all basically the same, but by the late 1970s and early '80s their individual plots had developed some originality. Here are some of the others.

Gowappa 5 Godam

36 episodes | April 4, 1976 - December 29, 1976

Gowappa was the name of the team of five kids, and Godam was their giant robot. This was the first giant robot program with a girl leader rather than a boy. The Gowappas, led by Yoko Misaki, go on an outing to a strange island where they find the abandoned laboratory of Doctor Hoarai, who had been obsessed that the surface of Earth was about to be invaded by underground rock people. He was ridiculed, so he built the Godam giant robot and other weapons in secrecy to fight them. Before Hoarai died, he transferred his mind into a computer, and he convinces the five kids to take his place, with snazzy costumes and a super-vehicle for each. Yoko gets the A-plane, and the others are the Heli-Marine, the Yakodari Jeep, the Turtle Tank, and the Gasomachine.

Gowappa 5 Godam was not a comedy, but it was not very serious, either. The peppy theme song captures its mood nicely. Is it just me, or does Godam remind you of a giant robot pelican? Or a giant robot Jay Leno? The series was developed by Tatsunoko Productions.

Ga-Keen

Magne Robo Ga-Keen; Magnetic Robot Ga-Keen

39 episodes | September 5, 1976 - June 26, 1977

Doctor Kazuki builds a giant magnetic robot to fight the Izaru space invaders. Ga-Keen was short for "Gathering Keen", which meant its two parts that magnetically "gathered" together. Ga-Keen's two pilots were handsome Takeru Hojo and Dr. Kazuki's daughter Mai. When the two halves joined into one, the two pilots merged into one body. The prudish in both Japan and America thought that there was something risqué about a male and a female sharing the same body, which kept *Ga-Keen* from making a major sale in America.

Ga-Keen was produced by the Toei Animation Co., which did not rely solely on Go Nagai; instead, the series was planned by Kenji Yokoyama and developed by Masahisa Saeki and series director Tomoyoshi Katsumada.

Danguard Ace
Wakusei Robo Danguard Ace; Planetary Robot Danguard Ace
56 episodes | March 6, 1977 - March 26, 1978

Leiji Matsumoto was very prestigious right after *Space Battleship Yamato* and *Space Pirate Captain Harlock*, and so Toei Animation invited him to come up with something in the giant robot genre.

In the future, Earth has exhausted its natural resources and must be abandoned. The authorities plan to evacuate Earth for the planet Promete (Prometheus), but the ultra-wealthy Mr. Doppler flies to Prometheus in his own spaceship, uses his wealth and Prometheus' resources to construct a private army, and declares himself chancellor of Prometheus. The Earth governments begin to build giant robots to defeat him, but Doppler's agents destroy them before they are finished— except for Danguard Ace. The series is set on the Earth fleet approaching Prometheus, under the command of the mysterious masked Captain Dan, fighting the concentrated forces of Doppler with Danguard Ace. The protagonist is Takuma Ichimonji, the young pilot of the Danguard Ace, whose father is believed to have defected to Doppler.

Daitan 3
Muteki Kojin Daitan 3; Invincible Steel Man Daitan 3
40 episodes | June 3, 1978 - March 31, 1979

Imagine Batman with a giant robot instead of the Batmobile. Imagine that Bruce Wayne (Banjo Haran) really is an ultra-wealthy playboy who spends his time, when not fighting the evil Martian cyborgs who killed his scientist parents, at swanky cocktail parties surrounded by two gorgeous women, Reika and Beauty. "Hey, baby, wanna take a spin in my giant robot?" His Alfred-like butler is named Garrison. "Garrison, I don't feel like fighting the Meganoids tonight. Why don't you take Daitan 3 out in my place?" "Veddy good, sir." There is a Robin-like young orphan, too.

Daitan 3 was notable for giving each Meganoid an individual personality and intelligent dialogue, when all other giant robot programs treated their main villains' minions as cookie-cutter cannon-fodder. An imaginative series by Nippon Sunrise, which would go on to still better things.

Gordian
Toshi Gordian; Warrior Gordian
73 episodes | October 7, 1979 - February 27, 1981

In the near future, Earth has become a desert wasteland except where survivors are struggling to rebuild small towns. Daigo Otaki is a young man raised alone by his uncle. When he becomes an adult, he sets out across the desert on his motorcycle, with Clint, his robot black panther, for Victor City, where his father is said to be. Daigo finds that Victor City is a paradise amidst the wasteland, mostly built by his father who was a super-scientist, but it is under siege by the criminal Makudoka organization. Victor City's defense has been led by Saori, his sister whom he didn't know he had. She begs him to take over Victor City's defense with his father's inventions, which only he can use. He joins the Mechacon Mechanic Combat's 18th regiment unit to help it out while learning to use his father's inventions. The principal invention is a robot battle suit named Protteser. When Daigo gets into too much trouble for Protteser to handle, they get into a bigger battle suit named Delinger, then another named Garbin. When all appears lost, Gordian appears as an autonomous giant robot deus ex machina to save them. Gordian is developed as a mystery: first, who Daigo and his robot panther are, then who the invaders are and what they want, and finally what Gordian is and what commands it is operating under.

Gordian was credited to Tatsunoko Pro's founder, Tatsuo Yoshida, who died in 1975, making you wonder how long it was in development. The most popular toys were the three increasing-sized battle suits. I always suspected that they were inspired by Russian nesting dolls (matryoshkas).

Trider-G7
Muteki Robo Trider-G7; Invincible Robot Trider-G7
50 episodes | February 2, 1980 - January 24, 1981

Businessman Uo Takeo, collaborating with a renegade scientist from the evil Robot Empire, builds the Trider-G7 to defend Earth. As a cover identity, Takeo claims to have built Trider-G7 himself for commercial purposes, and forms a shell company pretending to rent it out as a super-bulldozer or steam shovel, with himself as the pilot. He is unexpectedly killed in an accident while his son Watta is too young to run it, with his unaware shell company taking itself seriously. Watta is just being trained by the Takeo General Company's employees—the office secretary, the mechanic, the mailroom boy, even the Takeo family butler—when the Robot Empire strikes. Trider-G7 is Earth's only hope for defense, and Watta needs to pilot it Right Now!

Trider-G7 was not exactly a comedy, but its emphasis was less on the giant robot battles and the villains than on how being a giant robot's pilot affected an enthusiastic but untrained elementary-school kid. Watta was always being called out from class or in the middle of a baseball game to fly Trider-G7 against some new menace. His classmates thought that being a giant robot pilot was cool! When he powered up the robot, everyone in the neighborhood could watch. I felt that if any Japanese TV cartoon would have been perfect for an American live-action adaptation, it would have been *Trider-G7*, with a child actor like Jon Provost (Timmy on *Lassie*) as Watta, and Edward Everett Horton as the grumpy but lovable old family butler. From Nippon Sunrise.

Daioja
Saikyou Robo Daioja; Robot King Daioja
50 episodes | January 31, 1981 - January 30, 1982
In the far future, 16-year-old Crown Prince Mito of the galactic Empire of Edon makes a tour of his future realm with his two bodyguards/pals, Kurks and Skade, all disguised as teenaged commoners. They are just supposed to observe, but if they run across any crimes, they have the giant robot Daioja (literally "Big Prince") to punish the evildoers. They are trailed by the girl spy Shinobu (a futuristic ninja) who is secretly assigned by the king to keep them out of more trouble than they can handle, and to report on what kind of ruler Mito shows that he will make.

Daioja was a pastiche of the fantastically popular Japanese live-action drama *Mito Komon*, on TV from 1969 to 2011. *Mito Komon* was a period drama set in 17th-century Japan, about an elderly vice-shogun who disguised himself as a retired crêpe merchant; *Daioja* updated the plot into s-f with a teen hero, and was played for low comedy and bad puns. In one episode, Mito finds that a tyrannical planetary governor who fancies himself a Patron of the Arts has ordered the commoners to play living statues of famous works of art like the Mona Lisa and Rodin's "The Thinker", for the rest of their lives. He stations guards with guns near them, so the first time that they break their poses, that's the rest of their lives. When Mito reveals his true identity and shouts, "You have betrayed your trust! You have lost face!", the governor pulls out a hand mirror and says, "What do you mean, I have lost my face? It's still here." (Groan!) From Nippon Sunrise.

Gold Lightan
Ogon Senshi Gold Lightan; Golden Warrior Gold Lightan
52 episodes, March 1, 1981, to February 18, 1982
A boy, Hiro Taikai, finds what appears to be a gold Zippo cigarette lighter,

but which transforms into the Gold Lightan giant robot. He has just been sent to Earth with his nine teammates, all giant robots which can shrink and disguise themselves as small household tools (magnifying glass, pencil sharpener, etc.), to defend the planet against an invasion by King Ibalda's alien robots. Hiro and his pals, as the Bratty Rangers Club, each take a device/robot.

Gold Lightan was a serious drama, but you can't tell me that the Tatsunoko animation team was serious. It was rumored that someone challenged each of the animators to take some small object from his pockets or desk, and then work them all together into a giant robot scenario. Gold Lightan's being an obvious and well-known cigarette lighter kept this off American television. This was not one of the giant machines with a human pilot, but I couldn't resist telling you about the giant gold cigarette lighter. The toy, which looked like a real Zippo but transformed into a miniature robot, sold for something like $85 in L.A.'s Japanese community toy shops.

God Mars
Rokushin Gattai God Mars; Six God Combination, or Hexademon
64 episodes | October 2, 1981 - December 24, 1982

In 1999, evil Emperor Zul of the planet Gishin plots to conquer the universe, but he fears that Earth, which has just developed space travel, may oppose him. He secretly sends a baby, Mars, to Earth to grow up as a human, with a giant robot, Gaia, built by Mars' father, which contains a super-bomb that can destroy the planet. Zul plans that if he cannot conquer Earth while Mars grows up, he will order Mars to destroy it. However, the baby Mars is adopted by a Japanese family who name him Takeru, and he grows up believing himself to be human. When Zul reveals Mars' true identity when the boy is 17 and orders him to destroy Earth, Mars decides to fight for his adopted planet. He joins the Crasher Squad defending Earth from Zul's attacks. However, if Mars dies, the bomb with Gaia will explode automatically, so Zul constantly tries to kill Mars. What Zul does not realize is that Mars' father built six more robots to protect him. Mars uses the six robots to defend Earth from Gaia. The six can combine into the God Mars super-robot. From Tokyo Movie Shinsha.

Acrobunch
Makyo Dentetsu Acrobunch; Acrobunch: The Legend of the Demon Lands
24 episodes | May 5, 1982 - December 24, 1982

The series was so-named because Acrobunch was a giant robot piloted by a bunch of acrobats. Seriously. Tatsuya Randou, the leader of the Randou family of circus acrobats, is also a scientist and archaeologist in his spare time. He unearths evidence of a fabulous Quetzalcoatl treasure, which can be located by clues in the ruins of lost civilizations all over Earth. The Randous set out in their Acrobunch to discover them, but they are trailed by the evil Gopurin organization which plans to seize the treasure.

Acrobunch took its archaeology very seriously, with detailed realistic designs. From Tokyo Movie Shinsha.

That is ten more, with dozens to come. I could go on indefinitely. Someone made for YouTube a compilation of "[a]n almost complete collection of giant robot anime TV openings from the 1980s". Just the 1980s. It runs almost 80 minutes.

The "Real" Giant Robots

Anime fandom in America, at least in Los Angeles, was founded on the anime giant robot TV cartoons—the individual giant, almost godlike, robots that were heroes themselves, and that could only be piloted by a specific human hero (or heroes in the case of two or more smaller robots combining into a huge one). From 1976 to the early 1980s, we watched over a dozen TV programs that were variations of this stereotype.

We did not notice it when the first major change in this stereotype occurred, with *Mobile Suit Gundam*. The first episode was shown on Japanese TV in April 1979, but it was not shown on American TV. I think that we got our first video copies in early 1982.

These TV cartoons really blossomed forth in the early 1980s. The difference was that these were called "real robot" programs with battle armor or battle suits, not "super/giant robots". They were treated as ordinary military vehicles, like fighter aircraft, not special robots with a special pilot. Anyone with the necessary training could pilot one. Programs with battle armor featured more realistic s-f stories about futuristic warfare, not monsters or super-villains. They were noticeably more sophisticated, for older boys rather than children.

Because we focused on these programs, it seemed that the giant robots were almost all replaced by the battle suits in the 1980s. But the video compilations of all of the "mecha" TV cartoons in chronological order show that the giant robot TV cartoons actually still predominated. After all, the TV cartoons were really for the children, not the adolescents, and the children preferred more simple plots with robot superheroes and supervillains. But there have been enough "real robot" TV serials to overfill this chapter. Here are some of my favorites, ranging from the early days of anime fandom to the late 1990s.

Gundam

Kido Senshi Gundam; Mobile Suit Gundam

43 episodes | April 7, 1979 - January 26, 1980

Creator Yoshiyuki Tomino, at the Nippon Sunrise studio, really wanted to make a cartoon serialization of Robert A. Heinlein's s-f novel *Starship Troopers*, but the studio could not afford to license it, so Tomino wrote an original but similar story.

In the future, Universal Century year 0079, Earth is under one government and is surrounded by several Lagrange space colony habitats. One of them secedes as the militaristic Principality of Zeon, and begins a preemptive war of independence, relying on its revolutionary battle armor. *Mobile Suit Gundam* follows two teenage boys: Amuro Ray of the Earth Federation, a pacifist who refuses to fight until he is forced to, and Char Aznable, a Zeon charismatic fighter ace modeled on World War I's German Red Baron, in a scarlet battle suit. When Amuro's Side 7 orbital colony is attacked by Zeon, Amuro is among the evacuees in the Federation's White Base warship. As the White Base comes under attack and many of the evacuees and ship's crew are killed, Amuro finds the secret RX-78 Gundam prototype battle suit that the Federation has been developing, and becomes its pilot.

The sophisticated plot includes too many details and subplots to list here. Ironically, considering its later success (*Gundam* is considered a ¥50,000,000,000 annual property today), the anime serial was a failure at first, with such a small audience that the planned 52-episode story was cut back to 39 episodes. Nippon Sunrise persuaded the TV broadcaster and the toy sponsor to increase this to 43 episodes so the conclusion would not look too rushed. It was not until the 43 episodes were reedited into three theatrical features in 1981–82, the toy rights bought by Bandai, and the whole concept re-marketed for older boys and young adults instead of children, that *Gundam* became a major success.

Ironically again, fans in both Japan and America pleaded for years for a sequel. When Tomino was brought to the 1984 World Science Fiction Convention in Los Angeles as a special guest, and announced that Nippon Sunrise was finally developing one, there was wild applause. This was *Mobile Suit Zeta Gundam*, with an improved Gundam battle suit and an entire new cast—followed quickly by *Mobile Suit Gundam ZZ, V Gundam, G Gundam, Gundam W, Gundam X*, etc., etc., etc., plus lots more animated and live-action theatrical features and OAV mini-series, not to mention s-f novels, until *Gundam* has become a joke among anime fans. Most recently, *Mobile Suit Gundam AGE*, a 49-episode TV serial, ended on September 23, 2012, and *Gundam Build Fighters* began in October 2013. But the original series is still a massively admired classic.

Dougram
Taiyo no Kiba Dougram; Fang of the Sun Dougram
75 episodes | October 23, 1981 - March 25, 1983

"Not justice; I want to get truth!" The story, by Ryosuke Takahashi, opens with the wreck of the Dougram in the desert on the planet Deloyer, and develops as a flashback telling what happened.

In SC (Space Century) 140, political unrest on the desert colony planet Deloyer escalates into a war of independence from the tyrannical Earth Federation. The story follows teenage Crinn Cashim, the rebellious son of power-hungry Governor Denon Cashim who has the support of the Federation. Crinn joins a mostly teenaged guerilla team, the Deloyer 7, popularly known as the Fang of the Sun, fighting for Deloyer's independence. The Fang of the Sun have the prototype Dougram combat armor; the Federation troops use lots of inferior armors, mostly the Soltic H-8 Roundfacers.

Despite thirteen types of combat armor (with expensive toys of each of them), Takahashi and Nippon Sunrise developed a story that was light on expensive action scenes and heavy on political and military intrigue, with lots of talking-head conversations, telephone calls, conferences, and so on. The result was not much action but a complex, realistic political/military s-f drama.

Xabungle
Sento Meka Xabungle; Combat Mecha Xabungle
50 episodes | February 6, 1982 - January 29, 1983

This began as a lighthearted "space Western" by *Gundam* creator Yoshiyuki Tomino, and gradually grew more complex and serious.

On the planet Zora, presumably settled by humans who have forgotten their origins, civilization is fragmented and slowly running down. The Sand Rats, a gang of juvenile delinquents, meet a loner, Jiron Amos. They make him one of their team after he helps them out; he accepts to further his own goal of vengeance against Timp Shaloon, who murdered his parents a week ago. The Sand Rats are out to steal themselves some Walker Machines, all-purpose vehicles. Jiron hotwires a giant Xabungle model Walker Machine, used by the military. The Sand Rats use the Xabungle mainly for a home and team transportation. More common in Xabungle is the smaller Blue Gale personal Walker Machines.

This was one of the first anime series that noticeably began as lighthearted comedic action and gradually became more serious. Probably the extreme is the 1998 space-Western *Trigun*, which starts out as almost a slapstick comedy and ends up slit-your-wrists depressing.

Macross
Chojiku Yosai Macross; Super Dimension Fortress Macross
36 episodes | October 3, 1982 - June 26, 1983

In 1999 (then 16 years in the future), a humongously large robot war machine crashes on Earth. Ten years later, after learning to run the SDF-1, a bridge crew is assigned to take it into space for its breakdown cruise. They accidentally trigger a space-warp transition to Pluto orbit. Fearing to set off anything else, they take months to return to Earth by conventional power. They find Earth under attack by the Zentradi, giant humanoid aliens who have come after the SDF-1 Macross.

Macross was conceived as a parody of the giant robot genre, with a robot so large that a city could be built inside it. It was made more serious, and developed as a teen romantic triangle set against a space war, between young military pilot Hikaru Ichijo and two girls, Macross bridge officer Misa Hayase and Chinese pop-singer Lin Min Mei. Everyone lives within the Macross; the main individual battle armor are the popular VF-1 Valkyrie transforming fighter planes.

The series was fantastically popular. In Japan, the original TV anime was expanded from 26 to 39 episodes. It has been revived over thirty years in TV sequels, OAVs, and a theatrical feature. It was the first real-robot anime to become well-known in America, as the most popular component of the American-produced *Robotech,* which has had its own original sequels.

VOTOMS
Soko Kihei VOTOMS; Armored Trooper VOTOMS
52 episodes | April 1, 1983 - March 23, 1984

This series was created by Ryosuke Takahashi and Nippon Sunrise, and is very similar in mood to their Dougram although very different in plot.

In an interstellar war that has gone on for so long that nobody remembers why it began, a soldier named Chirico Cuvie, the pilot of a one-man Armored Trooper suit (officially a VOTOMS, for "Vertical One-man Tank for Offense and ManeuverS"), is set up for betrayal during a mission to capture a mysterious woman super-soldier, and left to die. He escapes from the Gilgamesh military into a seedy civilian world, and progressively moves to other cultures as he flees ahead of the military and criminal gangs. As he avoids capture, Chirico tries to learn about his own mysterious past, which may involve Fyana, the woman super-soldier. There are clues that both may be experimental super-soldiers or cyborgs, and may be immortal.

Giant Gorg

26 episodes | April 5, 1984 - September 27, 1984

I probably shouldn't include this here, but I can't resist. When mysterious Austral Island rises to the surface of the South Pacific, it is explored by Drs. Tagami from Japan and Wave from the U.S. It supposedly submerges again right away. Later when Dr. Tagami dies, he leaves a letter telling his young son Yuu to go to Dr. Wave in New York to learn the real secret of Austral Island. Yuu finds Dr. Wave and his younger sister Doris (who is Yuu's age) living in a New York slum, and targeted for murder by the GAIL megacorporation which is a major secret financial contributor to both Ronald Reagan and Yuri Andropov. GAIL has suppressed the fact that Austral Island is still there, and has sent a research team to discover its secret. Yuu, the Waves, and their small party go to Austral to beat GAIL to the secret.

We were halfway through Episode 3 when I started laughing hysterically. I had just recognized the plot by Yoshikazu Yasuhiko (who also did the character designs)—until they get to Austral Island, anyway—as a reversal of the first months of Milton Caniff's classic *Terry and the Pirates*. A plucky young Japanese orphan comes to exotic America to have adventures with colorful native characters. Instead of the Dragon Lady, there is Lady Lynx, the femme fatale boss of all the Las Vegas casinos. The NYC slum is realistically graffitied with background words like FUCK. Dr. Wave and his Great Dane Argus are comic-relief caricatures of Woody Allen and Scooby-Doo, a teamup that has to be seen to be believed. Each episode ends with the caption in English, "TUNE IN TO THE NEXT the same GORG time the same GORG channel", which made it obvious that one of Yasuhiko's influences was the campy 1966–68 *Batman* TV comedy.

I later learned that Nippon Sunrise was very proud of getting away with the first four episodes before the sponsor realized that their giant robot toy was not in it, and ordered the studio to include it from then on. Also, *Giant Gorg* was originally planned as a very short series—18 episodes, I think—and when it was more popular than expected, the studio was ordered to expand it to 26. This resulted in a lot of obvious padding, mostly in trekking around Austral Island and not finding Giant Gorg's secret.

Giant Gorg was never a battle suit. It was an intelligent artificial life form, not under anyone's control. Yuu did not enter into it; he rode either in Gorg's hand or in a cupola atop its head. Gorg usually did what Yuu wanted, but as though it was consciously agreeing to it rather than following orders. *Giant Gorg* was an intelligent and extremely likeable s-f serial (except for the episodes that were padding and did not go anywhere).

Let's jump ahead to some of the "real robot" TV anime series from the late 1980s and the 1990s.

Patlabor

Kido Keisatsu Patlabor; Mobile Police Patlabor

47 episodes | October 11, 1989 - September 26, 1990

Patlabor was produced by Sunrise, Inc., which changed its name from Nippon Sunrise in 1987. The series was also known as *Patlabor on Television,* to distinguish it from the earlier 7-episode OAV series whose popularity led to the TV series,

What if the police had battle armor instead of patrol cars? That's the premise of *Patlabor*, which stood for "Patrol Labor", a Labor being a battle suit used for heavy industrial and commercial purposes. In the near future, girl rookie Noa Izumi joins the Tokyo Metropolitan Police, Special Vehicle Section 2, Division 2—the Patlabor Division, comprised of six other officers and two mechanics. Besides Noa, there are Captain Kiichi Goto, a sleepy-looking but very sharp commander; Asuma Shinohara, the son of the president of Shinohara Heavy Industries, who joined the police force to prove that he can make it on his own without his father's influence; Isao Ohta, a loud male chauvinist pig, and proud of it; Mikiyasu Shinshi, the only married man in SV-2; and Hiromi Yamazaki, a "gentle giant". There are also several other regular supporting characters: the mechanics; Kanuka Clancy, temporarily attached to SV-2 from the NYPD to study the effectiveness of Labors for police work; the officers of SV-1; and so on.

Patlabor was very popular due to clever writing. All of the characters were intelligent (maybe except for the blustering Ohta). The cast may have been inspired in part by the cast of the popular American movie and TV series *M.A.S.H. Patlabor's* fans never knew what kind of episode to expect next; a realistic police drama, a soap opera about the off-duty lives of the members of SV-2; a police comedy like the *Naked Gun* series; a parody of Japanese monster movies; an anti-bureaucracy satire; or something else. *Patlabor* inspired three animated theatrical features, several OAVs, novels, and video games; a live-action feature is currently in preproduction.

Gasaraki

25 episodes | October 4, 1998 – March 28, 1999

This series, directed but not written by Ryosuke Takahashi for Sunrise, is set in the very near future. It involves a war between the United

Nations (mainly the U.S. Army) and the mythical Middle Eastern nation of Belgistan, and was clearly partially inspired by the Gulf War against Iraq. The main focus is upon the Japanese family-run Gowa Corporate Group of arms merchants. They sell military hardware to the Japanese Self Defense Force, and would really like to make the U.S. Army a customer. The Gowa family has just developed Tactical Armors (TAs), and Yushiro Gowa, a quiet teenager and the "omega" of the family, is assigned to demonstrate them to the JSDF. Suddenly, when the U.S. forces are about to capture Belgistan's capital, they are surprised and defeated by a new force using what appears to be TA technology. The Gowas rush to take advantage of this by presenting their TAs to the American military as superior, and getting the JSDF to deploy its team (including Yushiro) testing the TAs to Belgistan to try them out under real battlefield conditions.

Gasaraki mixes realistic modern Middle Eastern military action (with TAs instead of tanks and armored support vehicles) with the jockeying for power within the large Gowa family, and fictional but realistic Japanese politico-economic drama featuring the zaibatsu, the powerful families that manipulate and control the national economy. *Gasaraki* also contains elements of kabuki and noh theater, traditional Japanese mysticism including the Shinto religion, the modern role of samurai, and the mystery of what Gasuraki is. A suspenseful modern s-f drama, but deliberately mature, cynical, and depressing.

Dai-Guard

Chikyu Boei Kigyo Dai-Guard; Terrestrial Defense Corporation Dai Guard
26 episodes | October 5, 1999 - March 28, 2000

Hey, a "real robot" anime TV series by a studio other than Sunrise: the then-brand-new XEBEC, Inc.

In 2018, Japan is attacked by giant monsters called Heterodynes which conventional weapons are helpless against. The 21st Century Defense Security Corporation, under subcontract to the government, designs the Dai-Guard, a giant battle armor that takes three people to run it, to fight the Heterodynes. But before it can do so, the Heterodynes all disappear again. Left with a giant robot and nothing to fight, the military gives the Dai-Guard to its manufacturer in lieu of payment. Jump to 2030. Japan has been at peace for twelve years. The 21st CDS Corp. has not found anything better to do with Dai-Guard than to use it as a giant corporate mascot and advertisement, run by its Public Relation Division. The PR Division assigns three of its young office workers, Shunsuke Akagi, Ibuki Momoi, and Keiichiro Aoyama, to learn to pilot it and take it out for publicity jaunts.

While out at a seacoast security exposition with lots of tourists, a new

Heterodyne unexpectedly attacks, causing a panic. Hotheaded Akagi wants to use the Dai-Guard for what it was intended for, Ibuki dithers, and Aoyama says that he never expected to operate the Dai-Guard for real; he just wants to evacuate! But when women and children are about to be killed and nothing else can stop the Heterodyne, the others reluctantly listen to Akagi and power up the Dai-Guard. It is badly battered in the ensuing fight, but the Heterodyne is pushed back into the sea and vanishes.

Akagi assumes that they are heroes, but they are almost fired for using the Dai-Guard without authorization. Akagi is buried under a mountain of damage forms to fill out, and told that the cost of repairing the Dai-Guard will come out of his salary. Corporate executives tremble at the thought of damage claims and lawsuits against the company; and now that the Heterodynes have returned, the military wants the Dai-Guard back. Business rivals that never took the 21st CDS Corp. seriously before, now try to sabotage its operations. As Wikipedia says, "Dai-Guard's alien fighting soon begins to take a backseat to the bureaucratic troubles and office politics that the Corporation faces." The nominal giant robot gradually fades out of its own series to be replaced by the human drama.

The series ends with the public attitude shifting from demanding the Dai-Guard and the 21st CDS Corp. to permanently end the Heterodyne menace, to fatalistically looking upon the Heterodynes as disasters like earthquakes or volcanic eruptions, which must be combatted but can never be eliminated, and which are nobody's responsibility.

Chapter 2

加西生学由天谊 佛

Anime from 1990 to the Present

These dates are very loose, but basically this is a discussion of Japanese TV genres not tied to the introduction of anime to America.

Magical Little Witches

The first Japanese animation was theatrical, and meant for all audiences. The first TV animation was for adults (*Otogi Manga Calender*, 1962) and men and boys (*Astro Boy, Hermit Village*, 1963).

The first anime intended for girls was *Sally the Witch* in December 1966, followed almost immediately by *Princess Knight* in April 1967. Together, they established two of the three main forms of anime for girls: the magical little witch genre and the shojo-heroine genre.

Two famous examples of the shojo-heroine genre are *The Rose of Versailles* and *Revolutionary Girl Utena*; two more of the just-plain shojo are *Candy Candy* and *His and Her Circumstances*. However, there have been enough magical little witch series to fill this chapter alone.

Their original formula was that a young girl from a magic dimension would come to Earth and use her magic to appear to be a normal 8-12-year-old girl. She would use her magic secretly. Although she was a pre-adolescent, she would have adventures without any adult supervisor. When using her magic, there would be a "transformation scene" involving a magical phrase and some form of magic wand, often disguised as a locket, which would be one of the series' main merchandising tie-ins. The girl would usually have one or two magical animal companions.

As time went on, this formula developed many variants. The average girl grew older, from about 9 or 10 to about 14 or 15. Sometimes the girl was a normal human who controlled a magic object, but had to use it while avoiding being discovered by her parents or other adults. The most recent variant is the school for young witches in the magical world, where all the classmates have magical powers.

Sally the Witch
Maho Tsugai Sally
109 episodes | December 5, 1966 - December 30, 1968

Sally, the young Princess of Astoria, the Witch World, longs to visit the Human World. When she does transport herself there (an unnamed but obvious Tokyo), she meets two elementary school girls, Sumire-chan and Yo-chan, and uses her magic to become friends with them. When they are captured by two comic-relief burglars, Sally and Cub, another magical inhabitant from Astoria disguised as her little brother, play magical tricks to defeat them. Sally has such a good time that she decides to stay on Earth. She uses her magic to become Sally Yumeno, the daughter of a Tokyo family.

The program was adopted from the manga by Mitsuteru Yokoyama, the creator of *Gigantor*; he acknowledged the American TV program *Bewitched* as his inspiration. The program was also memorable for its theme song by Asei Kobayashi, in the style of Dixieland jazz. A sequel, *Sally the Witch 2*, in which an older Sally returns to Japan to look up her old friends and have new adventures, ran for 88 episodes from October 9, 1989, to September 23, 1991.

Akko-chan's Secret
Himitsu no Akko-chan
94 episodes | January 6, 1969 - October 26, 1970

Atsuko "Akko-chan" Kagami is an elementary-school girl who likes mirrors. For her devotion to them, the Queen of the Mirror Kingdom gives her a magic mirror and a spell that allows her to transform herself into whatever she wishes to be.

This was the first "magical little witch" series to feature a magical wand/object. It was remade into two TV series, with 61 episodes from January 9, 1988, to December 24, 1989, and 44 episodes from April 5, 1998, to February 28, 1989; two animated TV specials, or OAVs; and a live-action feature.

Magical Princess Minky Momo
Maho no Princess Minky Momo
63 episodes | March 18, 1982 - May 26, 1983

Fenarinarsa, "the land of dreams in the sky" where fairy-tale characters live, is in danger of disappearing because too many humans have lost their ability to dream and hope for a better future. The king and queen of Fenarinarsa send their daughter, Minky Momo, to help humans regain their dreams. She becomes the daughter of a childless couple, and goes about helping people regain their sense of wonder while accompanied by Sindbook the dog, Mocha the monkey, and Pipil the bird. There were numerous parallels with the Japanese folktake hero Momotaro, who was accompanied by animal companions. There were three OAV sequels in the 1980s and a new TV series with a new background story and supporting characters which ran for 65 episodes from October 2, 1991, to December 23, 1992.

Magical Princess Minky Momo was the first magical little witch program to feature a teenager instead of a pre-adolescent, and to feature her transforming into idealized adult women's occupations: a nurse, an airline stewardess, a policewoman, a soccer team manager, a saleswoman, a veterinarian, an explorer, etc.

Creamy Mami, the Magical Angel
Maho no Tenshi Creamy Mami
52 episodes | July 1, 1983 - June 29, 1984

Ten-year-old Yuu Morisawa is picked up by the spaceship of Pino Pino, a friendly alien. As thanks for Yuu's helping him, Pino Pino gives her a magic wand for one year which can turn her temporarily into a 16-year-old, and two alien talking cats, Posi and Nega, to be her guardians. Yuu, as the 16-year-old Creamy Mami, becomes a super-popular rock singer, managed by Parthenon Productions.

Creamy Mami was the first magical little witch TV anime to emphasize the problems of balancing a 10-year-old schoolgirl's life with the career of a mega-popular teen rock star, and to show the dark reality of the pop-star music industry.

Magical Emi, the Magic Star
Maho no Suta Magical Emi
38 episodes | June 7, 1985 - February 28, 1986

Mai Kazuki wants to become a master stage magician, like her mother who came from the famous Magic Carat Troupe. When Mai is frustrated by her juvenile inability to master complex adult stage illusions, the mirror fairy Topo gives her a magic bracelet that turns her into Magical Emi, a gifted teenage stage magician. Despite her success, Mai wants to learn to become a master stage magician without magical help.

Sailor Moon
Bishojo Senshi Sailor Moon; Sailor Soldier Team Sailor Moon)
46 episodes | March 7, 1992 - February 27, 1993

The original *Sailor Moon* was followed immediately by *Sailor Moon R*, with 43 episodes from March 6, 1993, to March 12, 1994; *Sailor Moon S*, with 38 episodes from March 19, 1994, to February 25, 1995; *Sailor*

Moon SuperS, with 39 episodes from March 4, 1995, to March 2, 1996; and *Sailor Stars*, with 34 episodes from March 9, 1996, to February 8, 1997.

Sailor Moon was the first series to combine the magical little witch formula with the boy's superhero team formula, with strong influences of the live-action "super sentai" costumed hero teams. Fourteen-year-old Usagi Tsukino, a typical boy-crazy teenager, meets Luna, a talking cat who tells her that she is the reincarnation of Sailor Moon, a magical warrior who saved Earth from various supervillains in the past. She must find the reincarnations of her teammates, and they must all battle the reincarnated villains while searching for the Moon Princess. The original team consists of Sailor Moon and Sailors Mars, Mercury, Jupiter, and Venus. Later additions are Sailors Uranus, Neptune, Pluto, and Saturn, and Usagi's daughter Chibiusa from the future. Each series features a different team of villains; the Dark Kingdom, the Black Moon Clan, the Death Busters, the Dead Moon Circus, and Shadow Galactica.

Sailor Moon was fantastically popular with young adolescent girls, generating three animated theatrical features, 25 stage musicals, a live-action 49-episode TV series, and numerous video games. In America, it was *Sailor Moon* that brought girls into anime fandom.

Cardcaptor Sakura

70 episodes | April 7, 1998 - March 21, 2000

Ten-year-old Sakura Kinamoto accidentally releases a magical deck of Tarot-like "Clow Cards" which escape separately around the city. Cerberus, the magical guardian of the book that they were imprisoned in, takes the form of a cute lionlike plush doll and tells Sakura that it is her duty to recapture them. *Cardcaptor Sakura* was notable for giving Sakura lots of human help from people who are aware of her identity, from her best friend Tomoyo, who video-films her battles with the Clow Cards and makes superheroine costumes for her (which Sakura will not wear), to her teacher and her older brother.

Cardcaptor Sakura was famous in Japan as the first magical little witch series developed by CLAMP, the popular team of all-women manga authors and artists. The manga by CLAMP and the TV series by Studio Madhouse got very good reviews. By 2000, Americans were well aware of the Japanese origins of dramatic animated TV series, and when the licensed American version, *Cardcaptors*, turned out to be heavily and haphazardly edited, there were strident demands from American fans for the original Japanese program.

Tokyo Mew Mew

52 episodes | April 6, 2002 - March 29, 2003

Twelve-year-old Ichigo Momomiya attends an exhibit on endangered species with her boyfriend (she hopes) Masaya Aoyama. Shortly after leaving, Ichigo and four other girls are bathed in a strange light. The next day, she develops a cat's ears and tail, and superhuman abilities. She learns from two handsome teenagers, Ryo Shirogane and Keiichiro Akasaka, that she has been infused with the DNA of the almost-extinct Iriomote cat (less than 100 left) to become Mew Ichigo and fight chimera animals. These are Earth animals that have been deliberately infected with an alien virus and have become monsters, to aid in the conquest of Earth by the human descendants of the planet's former civilization which fled when Earth became too polluted, and have returned to reclaim the world. Ichigo is assigned to find the other four girls from the exhibit who are to become her teammates: Mint Aizawa (Mew Mint), infused with a blue lorikeet's DNA; Zakuro Fujiwara (gray wolf); Lettuce Midorikawa (finless porpoise); and Pudding Fong (golden lion tamarin). Ichigo is the Japanese for Strawberry, and Zakuro for Pomegranate—all the girls have names of components of fancy desserts.

Complications are that Ichigo has trouble persuading the other girls to accept her leadership; that, while the other girls were at the exhibit because of a genuine interest in endangered animals, she was only there to accompany Masaya; and that Kish, the most sympathetic of the aliens, falls in love with her. Ryo and Keiichiro help the girls establish a cover identity and secret headquarters as Café Mew Mew, an exclusive tea shoppe where they pose as waitresses.

See also the entry for *Tokyo Mew Mew* in "Cat Girls".

Magical Witch Punie-chan

Eight 12-minute OAVs | March 3, 2006 - October 21, 2008

It had to happen: a super-violent NSFW burlesque of the magical little witch genre. This could not be shown on TV. Punie Tanaka is the princess of Magical Land who, to succeed to the throne, must become a transfer student to a Japanese high school for a year. Not only are the teachers sadistic and the students mostly juvenile delinquents, she has many rivals from Magical Land who want to eliminate her as the heir. One is Paya-tan, the little dog with a unicorn's horn who is Punie's cute animal companion to her face but who tries to assassinate her behind her back. Punie appears to be a sweet young girl until she gets into a fight—many of which she starts; then she unleashes her martial arts and her magic with extreme graphic prejudice.

There are lots of other magical little witch TV series that I could list, such as *Maho no Mako-chan/Magical Miss Mako, Fushigi na Melmo/Marvelous Melmo, Maho Tsukai Chappy/Chappy the Magician, Miracle Shojo Limit-chan/Limit-chan the Miracle Girl, Majokko Meg-chan/Meg-chan the Witch Girl,* and *Maho Shojo Lalabelle/Lalabelle the Magic Girl.* And that's just through 1980! However, here are two recent (early 2000s) variants of the formula:

Sugar, a Little Snow Fairy
Chitchana Yukitsukai Sugar
24 episodes | October 2, 2001 - March 26, 2002

Saga Bergman is a very orderly 11-year-old girl in a picturesque small German village. One day she finds a miniature little girl who is starving, whom she gives a waffle. The doll-like girl is Sugar, a 9-year-old apprentice season fairy who makes snow in winter. She has two friends: Salt, who makes sunshine, and Pepper, who makes breezes and windstorms. The three fairies are horrified to realize that Saga can see them, and make her promise not to tell any humans. The well-meaning but disorganized Sugar moves into Saga's bedroom, creating a juvenile "odd couple" situation. Saga's life becomes more complicated when more season-weather fairies show up in Muhlenberg, including three adults.

Sugar is a stereotype of the well-meaning friend who cannot be dissuaded from "helping out" magically, with disastrous results that Saga must hide from her human friends and adults. Since many of the magical accidents are caused by Sugar trying to help Saga, this is a form of magical little witches.

Alice's Magic Witch Squad
Maho Shojo Tai Arisu
40 episodes | April 9, 2004 - March 25, 2005

Eleven-year-old tomboyish Alice is bored with the world and thinks how nice it would be to be a witch. She is transported to a world where everyone BUT her is a witch. She is imprisoned after being mistaken for a renegade witch schoolgirl. When she finally convinces the authorities that she is a magicless human, she is enrolled in an elementary school for apprentice witches and assigned apprentices Eva and Shiela to teach her magic. The rebellious Alice gets them all into trouble.

This series is a witty reversal of the standard formula. The licensed American DVD by Media Blasters was called *The Adventures of Tweeny Witches*, or just *Tweeny Witches*.

The first series where three ordinary children get magic powers was *Magical DoReMi/Ojamajo DoReMi* (*DoReMi, the Useless Witch*), with 51 episodes aired from February 7, 1999, to January 31, 2000. This series was less interesting than *Alice*, in my opinion (the children are 8 years old), but as the first, *Ojamajo DoReMi* was followed by TV sequels, theatrical featurettes, and OAVs.

One of the most recent is *Little Witch Academia*, from new Japanese Studio TRIGGER, which released a first episode theatrically in March 2013. Later that year, in July-August 2013, the studio raised enough funding through Kickstarter ($625,518 of a $150,000 goal) to produce its second episode. Check it out on YouTube; it's good.

Other series in the category of "Magical Little Witches" are *Cutey Honey*, Go Nagai's parody of the magical witch formula, for lusty adolescent boys, and *Majokko Tickle* (*Tickle the Witch Girl*), Go's serious contribution to the genre. I discussed both in a previous chapter, "The Many Program of Go Nagai". In addition, see *Hana no Ko Lun Lun* (*Lun Lun, the Flower Child*), which I discussed in "Anime Fandom in North America, Part 2".

The Japanese magical little witch genre has become so popular that it has inspired original magical little witch TV cartoons in America and in Europe, such as the American Greeting Corporation's *Lady Lovely Locks and the Pixietails* (animation by DiC Entertainment in 1987); Saban Entertainment's *Tenko and the Guardians of the Magic* (1995–96); and Disney Italia's *W.I.T.C.H.,* begun as an Italian comic-book series from 2001 to 2012, and animated by SIP Animation in Paris, with 52 episodes from 2004 to 2006 broadcast or released on DVD around the world, including the U.S. and Canada.

Super Sentai Shows

The "super sentai (team) shows" all have a cartoony aura about them. When the Cartoon/Fantasy Organization began in May 1977, we did not watch only Japanese TV anime. We also sampled the Japanese TV live-action superhero programs. We found that these were hilariously campy, yet we quickly tired of them. After about a year, the C/FO was exclusively watching anime. What was exciting in anime was just silly in live-action; also, all of the live-action superhero programs were deliberately campy.

There was a predecessor of the live-action superhero TV series—what we learned were called in Japan the super sentai shows, a mixture of the English "super" and the Japanese "sentai", meaning a team or squad—that had been shown on American TV: **Ultraman**. Most anime fans had seen at least an episode or two of *Ultraman*, and those who'd liked it had watched it regularly. The series, which ran for 39 episodes, had originally appeared on Japanese TV from July 1966 to April 1967; it appeared on syndicated American TV dubbed by Peter Fernandez, Corinne Orr, and the *Speed Racer* crew, from approximately 1968 to 1972. It was produced by Tsuburaya Productions, a studio founded in 1963 by Eiji Tsuburaya, the man who had created Godzilla, Mothra, Ghidrah, and similar "men in rubber suit" live-action monster theatrical features for Toho Co., Ltd., the major Japanese theatrical film producer/ distributor during the 1950s. *Ultraman* had a forerunner on Japanese TV, *Ultra Q*, which did not appear on American TV; so for Americans, *Ultraman* pioneered the live-action "monster of the week who has to be stopped from stomping Tokyo" TV series.

Ultraman was so popular in Japan that as soon as it ended, it was replaced by the first of a series of sequels (in fact, if not in story), all produced by Tsuburaya Productions for the TBS (Tokyo Broadcasting System): *Ultra Seven, Ultraman Jack, Ultraman Ace, Ultraman Taro*, and a seemingly unending flow of others. By the time we started the C/ FO in 1977, Toei Co., Ltd. (Toei Doga, which produced animation, was a semi-independent subsidiary of the larger Toei Co. which produced and distributed live-action theatrical and TV films) was just starting its rival series of "super sentai" programs, designed by cartoonist Shotaro Ishi(no)mori's Ishimori Production Co, Ltd., for the NET channel (now TV Asahi), starting with *Go Ranger (The Five Rangers)*.

Go Ranger
Himitsu Sentai Go Ranger; Secret Task Force/Squad Five Rangers
84 episodes (plus several movies) | April 5, 1975 - March 26, 1977

An extremely popular series, running on TV for 84 weeks, *Go Ranger* established the super sentai formula of a team of color-coded superheroes working for a world police force and fighting an evil organization trying to take over Earth. The team always consists of three or four guys and one cute girl. In *Go Ranger*, it was Red Ranger, Blue Ranger, Yellow Ranger, Green Ranger, and Pink Ranger (guess which was the girl), members of EAGLE (Earth Guard League), fighting the supervillains of the Black Cross Army.

Go Ranger was among the first TV programs that the C/FO got in video-trade with fans in Japan, from Japanese TV; in other words, without subtitles. We had to guess what was going on, which was fairly easy because the acting was helpfully broad. Red Ranger was the leader, Blue Ranger was his loyal second-in-command, Green Ranger was the rash/ loose cannon of the team, Yellow Ranger was the comedy relief, and Pink Ranger looked pretty. The supervillains were ridiculous. My favorite villain-of-the-week was the one that I called Choo-Choo-Head; he had an old-fashioned steam locomotive with an evil glare for a head. He literally ran about the streets of Tokyo chuffing away, and it was easy to tell that the crowds of pedestrians were real pedestrians who were instructed by the camera crew to pretend that they didn't notice him or the costumed heroes pursuing him. Some of the crowd were better at keeping straight faces than others. (According to SuperSentai.com, this was episode #46, "Black Super Express! Locomotive Mask's Big Rampage", and the villain's actual name was Locomotive Mask.) Yellow Ranger was the only team member to be killed in action, by the evil Can Opener Mask.

Go Ranger was so popular that it was rumored, and believed, that the real reason it ended and was immediately replaced by *J.A.K.Q.* was that the sponsors felt that the market for *Go Ranger* merchandise was saturated, and it was time to move on to a new TV superhero series with new costumes, vehicles, and weapons for toys, action figures, etc.

J.A.K.Q.

J.A.K.Q. Dengekitai; J.A.K.Q. Blitzkreig

35 episodes | April 2 - December 24, 1977

J.A.K.Q. was one of the few super sentai shows that had only four members instead of five, but the Ishimori team was limited by a plot that had its superhero team looking like the Jack (diamond, blue), Ace (spade, red), King (clover, green), and Queen (heart, pink) of a card deck. They worked for ISSIS, the International Science Special Investigation Squad, and took orders from Commander Joker (rainbow). They fought Crime, a global criminal organization led by Iron Claw.

Battle Fever J

52 episodes | February 3, 1979 - January 26, 1980

This team had five superheroes with face-concealing costumes inspired by leading nations of the day: Battle Japan (the leader, naturally), Battle France, Battle Cossack (Soviet Union), Battle Kenya, and—ta-dah!—Miss America. They were from the National Defense Ministry, and they opposed the Egos Secret Society led by Satan Egos. This was the first super sentai show to have a giant robot or giant vehicle, the Battle Fever Robo. Miss America is really FBI agent Diane Martin (a Japanese actress), whose father was killed by Egos.

By this time, anime fans had had enough of the Japanese TV live-action superhero shows. Unlike anime, they were all identical except for superficialities like the costumes. We stuck with anime, with only a few live-action samples from time to time to make sure that we weren't missing anything good. When we were offered sample episodes of Japan's other mega-popular live-action TV superhero franchise, *Kamen Rider*, we said no, thanks (despite the fact that one of the Little Tokyo shops had a life-sized plaster Kamen Rider statue in front, who we called Potato-Bug Man for his insect-head mask).

For the record, here is a YouTube compilation that some fan made of the first dozen super sentai opening credits chronologically: *Go Ranger* (1975), *J.A.K.Q.* (1977), *Battle Fever J* (1979), *Denziman* (1980), *Sun Vulcan* (1981), *Goggle-V* (1982), *Dynaman* (1983), *Bioman* (1984), *Changeman* (1985), *Flashman* (1986), *Maskman* (1987), and *Liveman* (1988).

One live-action sample was of a superhero series that was not a sentai show: *Spider-Man*, which ran for 41 episodes from May 17, 1978, to March 14, 1979. *Spider-Man* was not made for TV Asahi, but it was a Toei production, at a time when Toei and Marvel Comics were working closely together. Toei Animation produced TV movie adaptations of Marvel's *Tomb of Dracula* and *The Monster of Frankenstein* comic books. The live-action Spider-Man wore the Marvel character's costume, but otherwise bore no relation to the Marvel story line. The Japanese Spidey is Takuya Yamashiro, a young motorcyclist who gets his powers from an alien with Spider Extract from the Spider Planet. He works with Interpol Secret Intelligence fighting Professor Monster's Iron Cross Army. He has a Spider Bracelet that contains his costume when he is not wearing it; he drives a flying car called the Spider Machine GP-7; he has a giant robot, Leopardon, that is really the alien's transforming Marveller spaceship ... all of these and more were available as toys, of course.

To establish that he is a Good Guy, Interpol helps create a teen hit dance, the "Spider-Man Boogie". Among the merchandise was an imitation of the John Williams *Star Wars* symphonic suite LP record, and a *Spider-Man* jazz symphonic suite arrangement of the series' opening and closing and incidental music by Michiaki Watanabe. I had Melody Records, a little Japanese-community music store, order me the LP from Japan; it was surprisingly good, with a full orchestra.

The major difference between this and the super sentai shows was that they were all played for laughs, while *Spider-Man* was done as dead-serious drama. Unfortunately, it just proved that a serious superhero action drama on a TV budget didn't work, not to mention that the obvious toy tie-ins were embarrassing. We watched a couple of episodes, and went back to the American Marvel comic book.

Anime fans were vaguely aware that Japanese TV followed up *Battle Fever J* with many other super sentai shows, but we didn't pay much attention until Saban Entertainment licensed the American rights and started bringing them to American TV in August 1993 as *Mighty*

Morphin' Power Rangers. We watched a few episodes, then returned to the anime. However, thanks to their popularity and fan internet sites, we know that Toei Co., Ltd. has produced 37 of them, from *Go Ranger* in 1975 to *Kyoryuger* (*Zyuden Sentai Kyoryuger; The Strong Dragon Powered Beast Team*) in 2013. There are six heroes now on the Kyoryuger (Strong/Powerful Dragon) Team: Kyoryu Red, Kyoryu Black, Kyoryu Blue, Kyoryu Green, Kyoryu Pink, and Kyoryu Gold. The evil Deboss Army invades Earth, and Wise God Torin sends heroes into the past to fight dragons (dinosaurs) to take their power and become the Kyoryuger to fight the Deboss. The Kyoryu Team appeared in two earlier super sentai series: *Zyuranger* (1992) and *Abaranger* (2003). Etc., etc. The information is out there for those who want it, and apparently a lot of adolescent Americans do, but they are not anime fans.

I confess that there is one that I watched a few episodes of: *Tokosou Sentai DekaRanger* (*The DekaRanger Special Police Team*), which ran for 50 episodes, February 15, 2004, to February 6, 2005. "S.P.D... Special Police DekaRanger. Five detectives who fight cool with burning hearts. Their mission: To combat space criminals who invaded Earth. They will protect the peace and safety of all humanity!" Four young humans in the city of Megalopolis are appointed by the Earth branch of the galactic S.P.D., under the command of Doggie Kruger (a bright blue wolfman alien in a bad fur suit), to fight crime. They are assigned cadet Banban Azaka, an alien teenage hotshot (whose superior is seen in a hologram to be Cthulhu-headed), to join the DekaRangers as Deka Red, but his arrogance turns off Deka Blue, Deka Green, and Deka Yellow. Deka Pink spends most of her time taking bubble baths with her three beloved rubber duckies. They are the DekaRangers because their supersuits, vehicles, and weapons are made of the S.P.D.'s special Deka Metal.

I was told about *DekaRanger* as a fan of anthropomorphized animals, because of Doggie Kruger and a very brief scene in episode #1, "Fireball Newcomer", where Deka Red, rushing from planet Chanbeena on his way to Earth, crashes through a Christian wedding ceremony of cat people. I watched this first episode and the next few, but there were no other animal aliens. I was mildly impressed, though, at how much Toei's live-action TV special effects had improved since *Go Ranger*.

After some of the material in this chapter appeared on Cartoon Research, I was accused of not knowing what I was talking about, for several reasons.

Firstly, there are many people who like the Japanese live-action superhero TV programs as much or more than the anime programs. To dismiss these programs *en masse* as more juvenile than anime, or as less popular than anime, is to imply that such programs as the Ultra series, the Kamen Rider series, or the *Mighty Morphin' Power Rangers* have little or no popularity in America, which is obviously not true.

Secondly, there are many fans of both. To imply that the fans of the anime programs and the fans of the live-action superhero programs are always different people is wrong.

Thirdly, it is wrong to imply that "super sentai" is the generic title of all of these programs. It refers to Toei's comedy live-action superhero teams only. The very term "super sentai" means a team or squadron or task force. Many of these TV programs outside of Toei's super-sentai shows feature lone heroes, and many are serious and even grim rather than comedic. The generic term for all of these programs, including the super-sentai shows, is "tokusatsu heroes", which translates as "special-effects heroes". In addition to the super-sentai or "fighting team" shows, these encompass the "kyodai hero" or "giant hero" shows that feature huge superheroes like the 40-meter-tall Ultraman, and the "henshin hero" or "transforming hero" shows that feature humans who turn into more than human (not just costumed) superheroes.

Obviously, there is more to the tokusatsu heroes than I said or implied. All that I can say is that the C/FO tried some of their episodes in the 1970s to the 1990s and 2000s, not just the blatantly comedic ones, and we were not impressed. Maybe we did not try a wide enough sample; but as I said above about the *Spider-Man* series, there was no way that you could produce a live-action costumed superhero program on a TV budget, especially considering the state of TV VFX in 1978–79, even if you played it for serious drama instead of comedy, without it looking silly.

Also, I have attended many American anime conventions from the 1990s to the present, including the massive Anime Expos and others before my stroke in 2005, and the smaller local Anime L.A.s afterward (mostly limited to day trips in my wheelchair). The thousands of fans there have shown interest in only the anime TV programs and theatrical movies, not in any of the tokusatsu heroes. I acknowledge that my description of the Japanese TV live-action SFX genre may have been oversimplified and incorrect in some details, but on the whole we will have to agree to disagree.

The Game Influence

TV anime was and is made primarily for children and adolescents. Everybody knew this. By the 1990s, children and adolescents were also getting increasingly…"addicted" is not too strong a word…to video games, also dominated by Japan. It was only natural that the two would combine. From the mid-1990s to the mid-2000s, American TV cartoon watchers—not anime fans, but "ordinary" American children—were the biggest fans of imported Japanese TV cartoons spawned by the gaming craze.

Anime TV series and OAVs based on Sega's *Sonic the Hedgehog* and Nintendo's *Super Mario Brothers* began in the early 1990s. Animated TV series about the *Sonic* cast actually began in America, from DiC Entertainment. However, this was seen as just a natural and very derivative merchandising of the video games.

The first TV and theatrical anime production that was seen as semi-independent of the video games that they were based upon was *Pokémon*, coming from Nintendo's 1996 *Pocket Monsters*. *Pocket Monsters*, quickly abbreviated by Japanese children into *Pokémon*, was an instant mega-hit, and the American 4kids Entertainment licensees decided to market it in America under its Japanese nickname.

It should be remembered that, in Japan, "monster" is any fantasy animal, including cute, little ones. The Western concept of a monster as only a huge, and probably dangerous or evil beast, does not exist.

Pokémon stood out from all previous video game-based scenarios by starting out with 150 characters ("Gotta Catch 'Em All!") instead of only one or two. The idea was for players to capture as many as possible of the cute, pocket-sized "monsters" (fantasy forest animals) in the game's pokeballs. 150 imaginary animals with no lead characters were unsuitable for merchandising that required a story line, so for *Pokémon*'s animated and comic book adventures, a 10-year-old aspiring Pokémon Master, Satoshi (Ash Ketchum in the American adaptation), named for the game's creator Satoshi Tajiri, was created, and one of the 150 Pokémon, Pikachu, the bright yellow electric mouse, became his personal pet.

Pokémon has been animated by OLM, Inc. (for Oriental Light & Magic), a Japanese studio created to animate the *Pokémon* franchise. The weekly TV anime began airing on April 1, 1997, and is still ongoing today with over 800 episodes, although technically it is a series of different programs and their sequels: *Pocket Monsters, Pocket Monsters: Advanced Generation, Pocket Monsters: Diamond & Pearl, Pocket Monsters: Best Wishes!,* and the most recent, *Pocket Monsters: XY.*

The story line is that, in the world of Pokémon, people compete to capture one each of the 150 (originally; more have been added over the years—there are 718 today) types of little creatures called "pocket monsters" because they are all pocket-sized, and train them to battle each other in League games. The original 150 Pokémon later came to be known as starter Pokémon. Those who capture Pokémon are called Pokémon trainers, and those who capture them all and win in their games are awarded the title of Pokémon Master. Children can leave home on their tenth birthday to roam the world hunting for Pokémon.

Ash Ketchum (to use the American names) sets out on his tenth birthday determined to become a Pokémon Master. His first Pokémon is the Pikachu electric mouse. However, unlike the other Pokémon hunters, Ash treats his Pokémon kindly and makes pets of them instead of training them to fight each other. Ash gains regular friends who accompany him, Misty and Brock, and regular enemies who try to sabotage him to advance themselves, Jessie and James of Team Rocket, with their crooked talking Pokémon, Meowth.

American anime fans began watching videotapes of *Pokémon* from the beginning, even though it was more juvenile than the usual anime-fan fare. The series had not yet come to American television when episode #38, "*Denno Senshi Porygon*" ("*Electric Soldier Porygon*", and one really suspects that the polygonal-sided Porygon was meant to be named Polygon), on December 16, 1997, sent "thousands" (later determined to be 635+) of Japanese children to hospitals with epileptic seizures. This drew headlines around the world, and editorials in American newspapers denounced dangerous Japanese animation. Mike Lazzo, the vice-president of programming for the Cartoon Network, was quoted in *USA Today* (December 19) as assuring the American public that dangerous TV cartoons like *Pokémon* would never be allowed on American television. One suspects that he was lying. The *Pokémon* TV series was a mega-hit, never mind the video games, and there was no way that the U.S. TV industry would ignore it. *Pokémon* began regular U.S. broadcasting on September 7, 1998, and it is still ongoing, from 1999 through 2008 on Kids' WB!, and since 2008 on the Cartoon Network.

The Japanese TV anime is also still ongoing, after almost twenty years. It was later determined that the 635+ children hospitalized had been watching TV in darkened rooms so closely that they almost got noseprints on the screen. The screen and the strobing lights in that episode had filled their fields of vision. Ever since, episodes of all TV anime programming have carried warnings to watch from a reasonable distance, in a well-lighted room.

The first *Pokémon* anime theatrical feature was *Pocket Monsters the Movie: Mewtwo Strikes Back*, released in Japan on July 18, 1998, and in America as *Pokémon: The First Movie* on November 10, 1999. I saw this as an animation-industry pro, not an anime fan; I covered the big premieres of this and the second theatrical feature, titled *Pocket Monsters the Movie:*

Revelation Lugia in Japan and *Pokémon: The Movie 2000* in America, at Grauman's/Mann's Chinese Theatre in Hollywood for *Animation Magazine*, and wrote articles about them: "*Pokémon* Graduates to the Big Screen" in *Animation Magazine*, November 1999, and "*Pokémon*: Ready for Its Next Success" in *Animation Magazine*, July/August 2000.

In Japan, a new *Pokémon* theatrical feature is still an annual summer event. The 16th *Pokémon* movie, *Pocket Monsters Best Wishes! The Movie: ExtremeSpeed Genesect: Mewtwo Awakens* (retitled for *America: Pokémon The Movie: Genesect and the Legend Awakened*), opened on July 13, 2013, and was the #2 grosser in Japan that week (the yen equivalent of $30,906,537). In America, however, the *Pokémon* movies went downhill fast. *Pokémon: The First Movie* had a big premiere at Grauman's Chinese Theater in Hollywood in November 1999; it was distributed by Warner Bros. in 3,043 theaters nationwide, and was the #1 grosser in America that weekend, earning a final box office of $163+ million, still the record for a Japanese theatrical animated feature in America. *Pokémon: The Movie 2000* also had a Hollywood premiere, on July 21, 2000, and was distributed by Warner Bros. It made a respectable $133,949,270, but this was noticeably less than the first movie despite increased advertising. *Pokémon 3: The Movie*, released on April 6, 2001, made only $17,052,128, and was the final nationwide release by Warner Bros. *Pokémon 4Ever* (2002) was distributed by 4Kids; it had a limited theatrical release but was mostly a home video release. *Pokémon Heroes* (2003) had an even more limited theatrical release before going to home video, and was the last to be given an American title instead of just translating the Japanese title. *Pokémon: Jirachi Wish Maker* (2004) was a home video release only, from Buena Vista Home Entertainment. By 2013, the *Pokémon* movie of the year appeared in America only as a two-hour Cartoon Network movie, under the English equivalent of its Japanese title, on October 19—not counting its later DVD release, of course.

Success breeds imitation. In Japan, where the *Pocket Monsters* video games and the TV anime on the TV Tokyo network were mega-hits, this success was not missed by rival game companies and TV networks. However, the only two that tried to create their own similar series were Bandai with *Digimon* (for *Digital Monsters*), with its TV anime appearing on Fuji TV, and Tecmo with *Monster Farm*, with its TV anime appearing on TBS (Tokyo Broadcasting System). In America, *Monster Farm* was renamed *Monster Rancher*. In both cases, the anime was just merchandise from the more popular video games, but it is all that is covered here.

In *Digimon*, seven children at summer camp are magically transported to the Digital World where digital creatures called Digimon live. Each of the children befriends a different Digimon, and discovers that he or she can help his Digimon partner evolve into an advanced form that can win battles against other Digimon. The children with their Digimon search for a way to return to Japan, eventually learning that they are "DigiDestined" to save the Digital World from a spreading evil. The *Digimon* anime actually began with a 20-minute theatrical featurette, on March 6, 1999, a day before the TV series that was its sequel. The TV anime lasted until March 26, 2000, with a second, 40-minute theatrical release on March 4, 2000, to advertise the TV series' coming end. In America, the two theatrical releases were combined into the 60-minute *Digimon: The Movie*, released on October 6, 2000. I also covered this for *Animation Magazine*, and wrote "Is Digimon Movie Destined for Success?" in its October 2000 issue.

In *Monster Rancher*, God sealed monsters into "disc stones" at some time in the dim past. Today, several of these disc stones have been rediscovered and the monsters released. Some people specialized in finding disc stones, releasing their monsters, and training them to fight each other. In the anime, *Monster Rancher* is the favorite video game of the boy Genki Sakura, who is transported into the Monster Rancher world. There he meets the girl Holly and the monster Suezo, a sarcastic big yellow eyeball, and soon after four more friendly monsters: Mocchi, a plump pink creature with green-scale "hair" that looks like the Japanese mochi pastry; the giant rocklike Golem; Tiger, the blue wolf; and Hare, the human-sized rabbit who is a martial-arts expert. The six Monster Rancher world natives, whom Genki joins and takes leadership of, are searching for the disc stone that contains the Phoenix. The Phoenix is rumored to be the only monster powerful enough to defeat Moo, an evil dragonlike monster who is turning all other monsters evil. The seven heroes are opposed by Moo and his henchmen, called the Big Bad Four in the American dub. There were no *Monster Rancher* theatrical releases. This title was unusual in retaining all the Japanese names of its cast instead of substituting American ones.

In America, both *Digimon: Digital Monsters* and *Monster Rancher* appeared on Fox Kids; *Digimon* from August 14, 1999, to July 14, 2003, and *Monster Rancher* from August 30, 1999, to December 27, 2001. This was promoted by Fox Kids as a part of its "Made in Japan" 4-hour cartoon block, along with *Megaman* and, later, *Flint the Time Detective*. On June 30, 2000, the block moved from Sunday morning to Friday afternoon, and was renamed "Anime Invasion". As the *Anime News Network* put it, "What makes 'Made In Japan' special is that it not only broadcasts anime, but that it makes no attempt to hide the country of origin. In fact, Fox Family embraces the origin of the series in many ways. 'Made In Japan' teaches simple Japanese words, and lists the current Top-3 Singles, Movies, and Video Games currently sold in Japan. In addition, they have trivia about anime and Japanese pop culture as bumpers between the anime shows and the commercials." This was certainly a far cry from twenty years earlier, when anime imported into America had to be marketed as original American productions to get syndicated TV sales.

Pokémon, Digimon, and *Monster Rancher* were the Big Three anime series based upon video games, but there was another that was based upon a collectible trading card game: *Yu-Gi-Oh!*

Ironically, *Yu-Gi-Oh!* (*Yugi, the Game King!*) began on September 30, 1996, as a manga by Kazuki Takahashi in *Weekly Shonen Jump* magazine, about Yugi Muto, a boy who was the champion of *Duel Monsters*, a complex trading card game to which every boy in the world was addicted. The manga was extremely popular, running weekly to June 2004, and merchandisers were quick to create a real *Yu-Gi-Oh! Trading Card Game*, and a TV anime series. In fact, there were two TV anime series due to the merchandisers' underestimating how long *Yu-Gi-Oh!*'s popularity would last: the first by Toei Doga, sponsored by Bandai, ran for 27 episodes on TV Asahi from April 4 to October 10, 1998, and the second, *Yu-Gi-Oh! Duel Monsters* by Studio Gallop and Nihon Ad Systems, sponsored by Konami, ran for 224 episodes on TV Tokyo from April 18, 2000, to September 29, 2004.

Yugi Muto is a shy high school freshman who is good at games. He solves the mysterious Millennium Puzzle, and is possessed by the spirit of a 5,000-year-old Egyptian pharaoh, known as Dark Yugi, from the puzzle. From then on, whenever a villain threatens Yugi or one of his friends, Yugi becomes Dark Yugi to defeat them at a game of *Duel Monsters*. The TV anime has several story arcs, involving Yugi vs. ruthless millionaires, or businessmen, or the owners of a rival game shop who try to sabotage Yugi's grandfather's game shop.

In America, the TV cartoons ran from September 29, 2001, to June 10, 2006, at first on Kids' WB and finally on the Cartoon Network. *Yu-Gi-Oh!* far outstripped *Pokémon* in creating a gambling mania. *Yu-Gi-Oh!* tournaments were held, and there were complaints from parent groups about the trading card game encouraging children to gamble away their lunch money, and encouraging gambling and cheating. At its peak of American popularity, its U.S. licensee, 4Kids Entertainment, commissioned the Japanese producers to make a theatrical feature, the 60-minute *Yu-Gi-Oh! the Movie: Pyramid of Light*, released on August 13, 2004 (November 3 in Japan, and ten minutes longer). I covered this for *Animation World Magazine,* writing "Yu-Gi-Oh! Anime Made ~~In~~ For America" in its August 2004 issue. Its premiere was not only at Grauman's Chinese Theatre, 4Kids Entertainment took over the nearest parking lot and set up a *Yu-Gi-Oh!* dueling trading card tournament for kids before the movie began.

After about 2006, American children went on to other fads, in TV animation and elsewhere. *Pokémon* has remained popular, but nothing like it used to be. *Digimon, Monster Rancher,* and *Yu-Gi-Oh!* are forgotten.

Those Fighting Virgins

One aspect of Japanese animation that the *gaijin* fan learns early on is that much of it exhibits Shinto influences, deliberately or subtly. For many early fans, it was the character of Benten in *Urusei Yatsura.* Many of space invader Lum's teenage friends from outer space were thinly-disguised Japanese mythological characters including Shinto divinities. Benten, a space-motorcycle-riding, swearing tomboyish gal-pal in a chain-mail bikini and with a bazooka, was based on Shichifukujin Benzaiten, one of Shintoism's Seven Lucky Gods. One of Benzaiten's divine aspects is Bishamonten, defender of the nation; hence, Benten's warrior appearance.

Almost any anime that involves a Shinto temple or shrine will feature that shrine's temple maiden as a prominent character. She is usually a close friend of the protagonist, and is usually the young teenage daughter of the shrine's hereditary chief priest. Examples are *Urusei Yatsura's* Sakura, who is also Tomobiki High's school nurse; *Kamichu's* Matsuri Saegusa, a junior high classmate of protagonist Yurie; and *InuYasha's* Kagome Higurasha, the 15-year-old daughter of the neighborhood shrine chief priest, who is the modern reincarnation of the shrine's 15th-century's warrior priestess, Kikyo.

Saint Tail, which ran for 43 episodes, October 12, 1995 - September 12, 1996, and was directed by Osamu Nabeshima at Tokyo Movie Shinsa, presents a bizarre, superficially Roman Catholic variant. Seira Mimori, a 13-year-old nun-in-training at St. Paulia's Private (Catholic) School who is the best friend of student Meimi Hanaoka, learns of people's problems, usually the result of their being victims of crimes, while hearing their confessions. She reports them to Meimi, who prays to God and is transformed into Saint Tail, in a costume based on a Las Vegas stage magician's assistant, to correct the injustice. Take my word for it; in Roman Catholicism, nuns do not hear confessions, especially not 13-year-old nuns-in-training!

Many of the ceremonies of Shintoism at the larger shrines are ritual dances, kagura, performed by groups of young virgin girls accompanied by traditional musical instruments. Before the end of World War II, when the powers of Shintoism were believed in more seriously, there were ritual dances to protect Japan from military defeat. Three anime productions, two by Ohji Hiroi or Ouji Hiroi, have been extrapolated from these beliefs.

Sakura Wars (*Sakura Taisen*) began as a Sega video game in 1996. It was so popular that it led to a six-episode OAV series (1997–1999, directed by Takaaki Ishiyama and produced by Studio Madhouse), a 25-episode TV series (April 8 to September 23, 2000, directed by Takashi Asami and produced by Madhouse), *Sakura Wars: The Movie* (85 minutes, December 22, 2001, directed by Mitsuru Hongo and produced by Production I.G), and more video games, OAVs, novels, and manga over the next half-dozen years.

Sakura Wars is set in an alternate history centered around Tokyo in the early 1920s. Japan is just recovering from the Demon Wars, an equivalent of World War I in which Earth, particularly Japan, was invaded by fearsome monsters. They were defeated, but everyone expects them to attack again soon. The Kanzaki Heavy Industries company in Tokyo has developed steam-powered battle suits to combat the monsters, but only soldiers with strong psychic energy can move them. To macho Japan's embarrassment, the only psychic recruits that can be found are young international virgin girls. The girls let the traditional military's dependence upon them go to their heads, painting their battle armor in bright pastel colors. The government organizes them into the Flower Brigade (Hanagumi), a secret battle group disguised as the Imperial Revue, a theatrical troupe similar to the real Takarazuka Revue. The Flower Brigade consists of their commander, Lieutenant Ichiro Ohgami, the only male with psychic energy (the stereotypical anime shy young man in charge of a group of uncontrollable adolescent girls), and the psychic virgins: Sumire Kanzaki, arrogant daughter of the president of the company that makes the battle suits; gun expert Maria Tachibana (Russian), mechanical genius Li Kohran (Chinese), telekinetic Iris de Chateaubriand (French, and nine years old with a teddy bear), martial-arts expert Kanna Kirisima (Okinawa), fingertip laser-beam shooting Orihime Soletta (Italian), and battlefield tactician Leni Milchstraße (German). Conflict is introduced when another Japanese girl, Sakura Shinguji, is found who has the psychic energy and is drafted into the Brigade. She just wants to help, but Kanzaki considers her to be a rival. When the Demon Lords of Death invade

Tokyo again, resulting in the fictional damage caused by the real 1923 earthquake that destroyed Tokyo, the squabbling girls have to learn to get along and fight effectively.

Besides the animation, the action figures and dolls of the girls in their individualistic bright-pastel 18th-century Western military officers' uniforms were very popular.

Virgin Fleet (*Seishoujo Kantai Virgin Fleet*; *Feminine Energy Naval Warfare Virgin Fleet*) aired as three 30-minute OAVs on April 25, 1998, July 25, 1998, and October 25, 1998. This minor production, directed by Masahiro Hosoda at the AIC (Anime International Company) studio, got almost unanimous negative reviews, but the premise is intriguing. The setting is an alternate world in which atomic power has not been developed, but Japanese research into paranormal mental powers has awakened psionic energy in some humans—but only young women, and only as long as they are virgins. Fifteen years earlier, in a conflict similar to World War II but supposedly a followup to the Russo-Japanese War of 1905, a ship of young women with this talent sunk a "federation" fleet about to invade Japan. This resulted in a cease-fire that has lasted to the present. A naval girls' academy, the Nakano Naval Academy, has been opened to train new girls with psychic "Virgin Energy" to crew a "Virgin Fleet" to protect Japan.

This is the background for a mostly silly teen farce. After fifteen years, Japan has been at peace for so long that the academy has turned into a finishing school where giggly teen girls play at being sailors and navy aviators. New student Shiokaze Umino has enrolled only to demonstrate she is still a virgin, to make a respectable bride for handsome naval cadet Mau Sakisaka. The academy's cadet leader Satsuki Yukimizawa, who is overly serious about the fleet's military mission, is determined to force Shiokaze out. The schoolgirl catfights (with Mau as a comically inept mediator) play into the hands of naval Chief Tatsugawa, a reactionary who has been trying to persuade the government to abandon the Virgin Fleet and rebuild the Imperial Navy. When enemy/Russian spies attempt to sabotage the Virgin Fleet in preparation to resuming the war, Satsuki is eager to put the Fleet into action at last, but she lacks enough Virgin Energy to be effective. Shiokaze has the energy, but she freezes in panic at the prospect of real danger.

What is most interesting about *Virgin Fleet* to me is the background portrayal of a Japan that has modernized without the dominating cultural influence of a Western occupation. There is technical modernization in appliances and the news media, but architecture and clothing styles are closer to those of 1940s Japan. The score by Masumi Ito is modern movie-music when punching up the action scenes, but in the style of traditional Japanese music in the street scenes. Even the opening and closing theme songs by Chisa Tanabe are pseudo-1940s or 1950s Japanese pop music, before it became as heavily Westernized as it is today.

Strike Witches began as a series of columns by Humikane Shimada in *Comp Ace*, a Japanese computer game magazine in 2005, and was made into novels, a 24-minute OAV, two animated TV series of 12 episodes each (2008 and 2010), and *Strike Witches: The Movie* (97 minutes, March 17, 2012). The TV and movie animation was directed by Kazuhiro Takamura, with animation of the first TV series produced by Studio Gonzo, and the rest by AIC.

As with *Sakura Wars, Strike Witches* is set in an alternate Earth with a major war replaced with a battle against demons, or otherworldly invaders. In this case, it is World War II. The countries are mostly transparent fictions of the nations on both sides in World War II, and the enemy is the Neuroi, whose weapons are really ominous CGI fighter aircraft. The Strike Witches are young girls from the world's armies who possess psychic energy and who are all assigned to the 501st Joint Fighter Wing in Britannia. Each Witch has a Striker Unit, mechanical leggings with propellers that enable her to fly and use her psychic energy to fight the Neuroi's aerial weapons. The anime concentrates on young Yoshika Miyafuji who joins the 501st Joint Fighter Wing. As an all-girl unit fighting unseen hive creatures, there is emphasis on the personality conflicts among the eleven international girls who are part of the Wing: Major Mio Sakamoto and Yoshika Miyafuji of Fuso (Japan); Commander Minna-Dietlinde Wilcke, Erika Hartmann, and Gertrud Barkhorn of Karlsland (Germany); Charlotte "Shirley" E. Yeager of Liberion (U.S.A.); Lynette Bishop of Britannia (Britain); Perrine H. Clostermann of Gallia (France); Francesca Lucchini of Romagna (Italy); Eila Ilmatar Juutilainen of Suomus (Finland); and Sanya V. Litvyak of Orussia (U.S.S.R.).

The first TV series is roughly equivalent to the 1940 Battle of Britain; the second TV series to the Allied conquest of Italy; and the theatrical feature to the Battle of the Bulge. *Strike Witches* emphasizes a different aspect of the nature of the psychic young women; late in the first TV series, Major Sakamoto begins to lose her psychic powers when she turns twenty, and becomes too old to be a teenage fighting virgin any more.

But this does not explain why they are such very young women, apparently of barely adolescent age (Yoshika looks nine or ten, though she's officially sixteen) with big breasts and bigger guns; or why using their psychic powers transforms them into dog- or rabbit- or cat-girls; or why there are so many crotch-and-panty shots and nude scenes. I have never seen an anime series with so much fan service; in some episodes the girls' boobs are almost bigger than their guns! And episode 7—NSFW! The first TV series was broadcast from July 4 to September 19, 2008, at 1:20 to 1:50 a.m. Obvious references to Shintoism, *Strike Witches* does NOT have!

Will Japanese animation be able to develop any further the theme of young women using psychic powers for military purposes? It seems unlikely, but it is such an unlikely theme in the first place....

Other Japanese Animation

Lost in Translation

When the Japanese animated TV series *Samurai Champloo* (26 episodes, May 20, 2004, to March 19, 2005) first appeared, most anime fans, both in America and in Japan, said, "That's an obvious misspelling. They mean 'Samurai Shampoo', whatever that's about."

Nope. It was quickly explained by producer Mangrove (Manglobe Inc.) that "champloo" is an Okinawan popular local stir-fry dish consisting of whatever ingredients are available to be thrown into it. *Samuri Champloo*, a gonzo samurai adventure-comedy set in 17th-century Japan with a hip-hop music score and such anachronisms as a six-shooter, American-style baseball, and Japanese bandits acting like Chicago gangsters, clearly threw "everything" into the stories. (*Samurai Champloo* was not the first TV anime to do this, but it was the first to do it in a "serious" rather than a slapstick format. See Charles Brubaker's comments about the 1967 *Pyun Pyun Maru* in his April 16, 2013, column on the Cartoon Research website.)

So that translation was accurate—rather, it did not need one. But what about other translations and transliterations? There have been some weird ones over the years.

One of the most popular of the early bootleg video tapes was Tokyo Movie Shinsha's (TMS) 1978 *Lupin III* animated feature. It was feature-length with theatrical-quality animation, and fandom got a tape of an English dub made for Japan Air Lines' in-flight movies, so the fans did not need to guess at untranslated dialogue. The main villain was the Frenchman Mamo, and his henchman was the hulking Flinch. To distinguish it from episodes of the *Lupin III* TV series, the C/FO's Mark Merlino referred to it as *Lupin III: The Mystery of Mamo*.

This went on for over ten years. Articles and reviews were written in anime fandom about the *Lupin III* TV series and *Lupin III: The Mystery of Mamo*. (Also *Lupin III: The Castle of Cagliostro*, but that was clearly the

Japanese title of the second movie.) In 1991, when I went to work at Streamline Pictures and I was asked for some fan-favorite anime that Streamline might license to release to the public, *Lupin III: The Mystery of Mamo* was among my first recommendations. TMS agreed, but for copyright reasons their American dub was not available. Streamline would have to redub it.

No problem, but when we got TMS' translation of the script, Mamo's name was spelled "Mamoux", and his henchman was Frenchy, not Flinch. Well, they were Frenchmen in gay Paree. The question was, should we keep the inaccurate American fannish spellings in our credits, or use the correct spellings and "tell the fans that they had been wrong for over ten years"? We opted to go with the established American spellings, partly because Streamline was already getting enough complaints from the fans about "inaccurate" translations—we knew that there would be screams that Streamline was changing the names of the characters. (When Streamline's license expired, TMS resold it as *Lupin III: The Secret of Mamo*. So the "Mamo" spelling has been kept.)

Actually, translating the title of the second *Lupin III* feature was not so straightforward. The Japanese title is *Lupin III: Cagliostro no Shiro*, which is literally *Lupin III: Cagliostro of Castle*. So which would be better in English: *Cagliostro Castle, Cagliostro's Castle*, or *The Castle of Cagliostro*? It was my argument that *The Castle of Cagliostro* sounded the most sinister. *Cagliostro Castle* is just a castle's name, like Windsor Castle, but *The Castle of Cagliostro* emphasizes that it is the evil Count's lair!

One of my jobs at Streamline Pictures was to check the pidgin-English translation that the Japanese licensees sent us when we acquired a new title, and correct it if necessary. This was usually straightforward enough, but once in 1992 I got into a big argument with Carl Macek, Streamline's boss, which I lost. We had just licensed an arty OAV titled *Manie-Manie* that consisted of three stories: a horror-fantasy directed by Rintarō about a little girl and her cat being invited to a creepy circus; a futuristic super-fast racing-car drama directed by Yoshiaki Kawajiri; and a sardonic comedy directed by Katsuhiro Otomo about a Japanese salaryman who is sent to a South American jungle site, where an army of robotic construction workers are building a new city, with instructions to stop production. *Manie-Manie* was meaningless, so we retitled it *Neo-Tokyo*. The first and third of the tryptich were "Labyrinth" and "The Order to Stop Construction", which were fine, but the Japanese notes said that the middle segment was "The Running Man". I argued that the correct title was "The Racing Man", since it was about a racing-car driver. But Carl overruled me and said that the difference was so minor that we should stick with what we had been told.

Many American fans turned out to be "more Japanese than the Japanese" regarding translation correctness. Anime fandom began in Japan at about the same time it began in America. Starting about 1978, Japanese publishers led by Tokuma Shoten (publisher of *Animage*, the first monthly serious magazine devoted to anime) began publishing books with extensive information on individual TV and theatrical anime productions. American fans bought imported copies that they couldn't read, just for the illustrations. (I remember the manager of Books Nippan in downtown Los Angeles complaining to me that young Anglo anime fans had started buying all of their anime books and magazines, leaving none for their regular Japanese customers. We cheered when Books Nippan's head office in Tokyo replaced her with a new L.A. manager, Yuji Hiramatsu, who ordered increased quantities and additional anime titles.)

Due to the Japanese penchant for throwing English phrases into all the Japanese text, even if it was broken English, the American fans soon became familiar with two of them: Roman Album and Perfect Collection. The Roman Album volumes were all published by Tokuma. "Roman" had nothing to do with the historic civilization in Italy; it was taken from the widespread European word for "romance", meaning fiction. The first Roman Album was on *Space Battleship Yamato* in 1978, and Tokuma is still publishing Roman Albums on current TV anime series today. Perfect Collection was a more generic phrase. Many publishers published Perfect Collections, and there were video collections of a series' episodes as well as books. One of the most prolific was Keibunsha's long-running series of pocket encyclopedias on animals, sports stars, airplanes, postage stamps—just about everything, with a new, updated edition every year throughout the 1980s. *The Complete Animation Encyclopedia* was volume 76 of Keibunsha's *Complete—Encyclopedia* series.

But the actual Japanese title of volume 76 was *Zen Anime Daihyakka*, and if you look up a translation of "zen", most dictionaries agree that it means "perfect; complete". Obviously, in this case, the Japanese publishers should have been using the second definition; these were Complete Collections, not Perfect Collections. But you couldn't tell the American fans! Perfect Collection it clearly said in English, so Perfect Collections they are. Today, after almost forty years, Roman Album and Perfect Collection are more widespread than ever, especially for new American productions. An American-produced 50th anniversary of *Godzilla* boxed set of all of the *Godzilla* movie music was a "soundtrack perfect collection". When award-winning cartoonist Shaenon Garrity publicized a Kickstarter campaign in 2011 to raise $10,000 to publish her internet comic strip in a printed collection, she announced it as *Narbonic: The Perfect Collection*. (She got $27,226.)

Ah, the notorious L and R confusion. Is the creator of *Space Pirate Captain Harlock* and *Galaxy Express 999* Leiji Matsumoto or Reiji Matsumoto? His name can be transliterated either way, and it didn't help that he thought it was funny to keep the American fans jumping by changing it back and forth. Finally, one of his publishers told him to pick one or the other and stick with it, and he chose Leiji. But there are still arguments over whether the English spelling of his popular space pirate should be Harlock or Herlock, similar to the four-way arguing among early anime fans over whether to spell his main enemy's name Laflesia or Lafresia or Raflesia or Rafresia, until it was discovered that Matsumoto had named her after the giant flower Rafflesia.

There is equal confusion over B and V. American fans chuckled when the Japanese studio Jin Productions was commissioned in 1982 to create an animated copy of Gerry Anderson's British "Supermarionation" TV series *Thunderbirds*. The result: *TechnoVoyager, the Scientific Rescue Team*. The Japanese had also tried for an allusion between Voyager and the mostly Boy team. It was good enough that after its Japanese TV run, it was dubbed into English by *Thunderbirds'* producer and shown on British TV as *Thunderbirds 2086*.

One translation that I am glad I didn't have to worry about was Nippon Animation's 1981–82 *Wanwan Sanjushi* (literally *Arf Arf Three Musketeers*), an adaptation of Alexandre Dumas' *The Three Musketeers* with a funny-animal cast, mostly dogs. This was actually commissioned from Nippon Animation by BRB Internacional in Spain for broadcast on Spanish TV; it was shown in Japan just because it was available. The Spanish title was *D'artacan y los Tres Mosqueperros*, a Spanish pun combining the Spanish words for musketeers and dogs: mosqueteros and perros.

How do you translate "mosqueperros" into English? This is not a theoretical question; the BBC licensed it for broadcast in Britain in 1985. How did the BBC translate the title? Literally, as *Dogtanian and the Three Muskehounds*. It sounds awfully clunky in English, but I could not have done any better. [Dwight Decker proposed "The Three Muttsketeers", which was so perfect that I was jealous of it.]

The film was so popular in Spain that BRB Internacional commissioned Nippon Animation to make another funny-animal adaptation of a French literary classic, Verne's *Around the World in Eighty Days*. In 1989 BRB commissioned an original sequel to *The Three Musketeers*, but from the Taiwanese animation studio Wang Film Production, not Nippon Animation. BRB claims that *Dogtanian and the Three Muskehounds* has played in more than a hundred countries in more than thirty different languages, and that a *Dogtanian* 3-D CGI feature is coming in 2014.

One suspects that many obvious errors have been caused by Japanese mistransliterations of English words by the American video licensees who were not as careful as we were at Streamline Pictures. Some examples: Lain's friend, "Arisu" (as in Wonderland) Mizuki, in *Serial Experiments Lain*. Or the Arisu of "Arisu's Magic Witch Squad" in some fan translations before Media Blasters licensed the series and translated it correctly. Arisu Fujisaki is also the name of a supporting character in CLAMP's *Angelic Layer*. However, it could be argued that all of these are cases of a popular English name given to Japanese girls, who would pronounce them in the Japanese way, like Mayo and Jun, character names in *Sol Bianca: the Legacy* that are clearly based on the months of the calendar. *Genesis of Aquarion* episode 9, "The Path of Dreams", is about children having their dreams stolen; its character Jun should probably be Jung. (A Soviet cosmonaut in *GunBuster* is named Jung Freud.) In *Galaxy Express 999*, episode 7, "The Graveyard at the Bottom of Gravity, part 1", the 999 sinks into the "Salgaso" (Sargasso) Sea of Space.

It should be noted that many of these anime titles' American licenses have expired, and they have been relicensed and retranslated by the new licensees, who may have caught and corrected the errors. So these errors may not exist in all versions, just like the first *Lupin III* movie has been called both *The Mystery of Mamo* and *The Secret of Mamo*.

Kosuke Fujishima's very popular manga *Aa! Megami-sama* has been published in English as *Oh! My Goddess*. The anime adaptation of it has been translated as *Ah! My Goddess*. (Fujishima says that "Oh!" is correct.) This has been going on since the 1980s.

One that nobody ever did figure out was in the *Dirty Pair* series, which ran for 26 episodes, July–December 1985, plus two OAVs, a theatrical feature, and a second TV series later in the 1980s. Kei and Yuri were two troubleshooters for the WWWA (Worlds Welfare Works Association) in the 22nd century, working under Chief Gooley. This was a fan favorite right from the start, so by the time Streamline Pictures licensed the OAVs in 1992-93, "everybody" knew the names of all the characters. One day we were talking with someone from Nippon Sunrise, the animation studio that had produced *Dirty Pair*, and I asked why they had picked Gooley as the name of the DP's boss? It was not a common family name in America or England. "Oh, but we named him after a famous American actor!" Huh? "Yes, he was the star in *The Music Man*!" Robert Goulet. When did he get the full name of "Andrew Francis Gooley" that's on the Dirty Pair Wiki today?

One series that probably cannot be translated literally is Go Nagai's horror-comedy *Dororon Enma-kun*, roughly equivalent to Harvey Comics' *Hot Stuff*, about the adventures of a child demon, Li'l Enma (the Prince of

Hell, actually; he's Satan's young nephew) in NYC or Tokyo or some generic human metropolis. I tried translating it as "Abracadabra! Enma-kun", but Nagai said, "No. He doesn't say a magic word when he casts a spell. 'Dororon' is the sound of the magic working." Er—is there an English word for that? This 1973 Toei TV anime is unsold in America, and the American release of a later OAV sequel cops out by calling it *Demon Prince Enma*.

And so it goes. I would like to thank Gilles Poitras for reminding me of a few of these that I had forgotten. In *GunBuster*, the name on the side of Noriko Takaya's father's spaceship varies between "Luxion" and "Lukyushiyon". There are *lots* of them!

Osamu Tezuka and Atomcat

Digital Manga Publishing (DMP) published the first American edition of Osamu Tezuka's manga *Atomcat* on June 25, 2013, with the title both ways on the cover: *Atomcat* and *A.Tomcat*. The pun is Tezuka's. I met him on several occasions between 1977 and 1986, a little over two years before his death, and he was very proud to be able to make puns like "A Tomcat" in English, which he did not speak.

One pun, or reference, that did not work out was his August 1978 TV movie *Bander Book*, Tezuka's version of *Star Wars*, which he showed at the Cartoon/Fantasy Organization early in 1979. It was about the interstellar adventures of a young hero, Bander. I told Tezuka that the title should have been in the possessive, *Bander's Book*. "But you say *Jungle Book*, not *Jungle's Book*! Why isn't it the same for Bander?" Another sort-of error was the August 1984 TV movie listed everywhere as *"Bagi, the Monster of Mighty Nature"*. Tezuka said that the intelligent cat-woman was deliberately named after Bagheera in *The Jungle Book*, so logically the title should be *Baghi, the Monster of Mighty Nature*. But the movie was unreleased in America or Britain, so a phonetic translation of "Bagi" in the title has become accepted as correct by everyone.

Tezuka originally considered Astro Boy, or Mighty Atom, to be "his baby". The first *Mighty Atom* manga story was published in April 1951 in *Shonen*, a monthly boys' magazine. Atom's adventures were serialized in stories of varying lengths throughout the 1950s. Tezuka later said that he was extremely gratified by all the fan mail that the stories generated; except that, after Isaac Asimov's science fiction began to be published in Japan, everyone started asking why Tezuka's stories did not follow Asimov's famous Three Laws of Robotics. Tezuka got tired of explaining that the Three Laws were just one author's gimmick for his own stories, not a rule that all s-f authors had to follow!

When Tezuka opened his own animation studio, Mushi Productions, in 1961 to produce TV animation based on his own manga, *Mighty Atom* was the obvious first choice. But Tezuka quickly found that what had been a pleasure became an onerous chore. Serials that had run in *Shonen* for almost a year were compressed into a single weekly half-hour episode for Fuji TV. Tezuka's backlog of ideas for future manga stories were almost immediately used up for TV episodes, and he was forced to grind out new stories mechanically. *Mighty Atom* ran weekly, first on Fuji TV and later on NHK, the government channel, for 193 episodes, from January 1, 1963, to December 31, 1966. In the final episode, Atom dies by flying a planet-destroying bomb into the sun, to save Earth. The last half of the half-hour episode consisted of tearful memorials and tributes to Atom from all his friends and world leaders. Tezuka was making sure that public demand could not resurrect Mighty Atom.

Tezuka's attitude toward Mighty Atom gradually changed to regarding him as just a commercial property. Tezuka wrote/drew one serious two-year serial from January 1967 to February 1969, *The Atom Chronicles*, for the *Sankei Shimbun* newspaper, a retrospective adventure reconciling all discrepancies and answering many years of fan comments. ("If Mighty Atom is always in favor of peace and against violence, why does he have machine guns built into his ass?") After that, Tezuka took it easy. When he was asked to draw a story showing Mighty Atom as a normal boy, Tezuka produced a two-pager showing what might have happened if Atom had not been programmed to be good, with him becoming a juvenile delinquent, shooting up drugs, and being arrested in a vice-house raid.

In 1980, the 1960s *Mighty Atom* TV series was so far in the past that Tezuka created a new TV series with state-of-the-art color animation. *The New Mighty Atom (Shin Tetsuwan Atom)*, which ran for 52 episodes from October 1, 1980, to December 23, 1981, was not a series of independent stories as was the 1963–1966 series, but a continuous serial that told Atom's life story as worked out in the late 1960s. It looked pretty, but it emphasized pathos over drama. Atom's love of peace was extended to the extent of turning him into a crybaby weeping for all the supporting characters who died tragically at the end of each episode. Tezuka pointed out in conversation with me that Atom was always *programmed* to be a "good boy", to avoid violence whenever possible; and therefore the new TV series made more logical sense than the 1963-1966 episodes. Maybe so, but as I said in an article, "Astro Old and Astro New", for the British *Manga Max* magazine, June 2000 (#18), "The black-and-white TV series may have been crudely produced, but it was imbued with a verve and sparkle which the prettier color remake almost completely lacked." The new series was received politely by the Japanese public, but it was quickly forgotten.

Tezuka was asked in 1986 by *Smile Comics*, a magazine for children, to create a series for it. He responded with *Atom Cat* (or *Atomcat*), *Mighty Atom* turned into a funny animal. It ran in *Smile Comics* from July 1986 to February 1987, and was clearly Tezuka's parody of his own most famous work. Tsugio, a shy schoolboy who is constantly picked upon by the school bully (named Gaddafi), is given a superscientifically-enhanced kitten by two honeymooning aliens. Atom finishes up Gaddafi and his gang, and becomes Tsugio's regular pet and bodyguard.

Atomcat was a trifle, quickly ended. The last time that I saw Tezuka, in August 1986 at Japan's National Science Fiction Convention, he jovially told me that he had just started a manga that I was sure to like, considering my other major interest in funny animals. Astro Boy as a cat!? WHY??? He chuckled and said something approximating, Why not? It was important to not take your work too seriously. Well, thanks to Digital Manga, now you can see it for yourself.

Anime Adaptations of American and British Lit

Japanese animation has introduced many Japanese historical events and cultural concepts to American popular culture. Contrariwise, many American, British, and other concepts have been introduced into Japan through animation. I will skip over the foreign-made animation shown in Japan, and the Japanese-produced adaptations of the better-known Western literary classics, and present instead some less likely others.

Agatha Christie's Great Detectives Poirot and Marple, a literal translation of アガサ・クリスティーの名探偵ポワロとマープル, consists of 39 half-hour episodes originally broadcast on NHK, the Japanese equivalent of the BBC, from July 4, 2004 to May 15, 2005, and still rerun frequently on NHK and other channels. It was directed by Naohito Takahashi for the animation studio Oriental Light and Magic.

The series is a generally faithful adaptation, set about 1930, of twenty of Christie's novels and short stories featuring her amateur detectives Hercule Poirot, the Belgian private detective living in England, and Miss Jane Marple, the English village spinster who "observes life". The adaptations vary in length, but take from one to two episodes for a short story and from three to four episodes for a novel.

There is certainly nothing unusual about a TV adaptation of Agatha Christie's mysteries—for adults. Where *Agatha Christie's Great Detectives Poirot and Marple* stands out is in NHK's linking the characters of Poirot and Miss Marple together, and making it a "family" program with an element to appeal to children as well as adults. The major innovation of the TV series is the addition of Maybelle West, Miss Marple's young and enthusiastic great-niece, who becomes Hercule Poirot's secretary and assistant to learn how to become a private detective herself. Maybelle (who every English-language summarizer of this program insists on spelling her name as the more prosaic "Mabel") has a pet duck, Oliver, who was doubtlessly added for the toy and plush doll merchandising potential. The mysteries are mostly told through Maybelle's observing of the cases during her employ with Poirot or her visits to Miss Marple, through the devise of her soliloquising and her letters to Miss Marple, which are usually Christie's own words, often as the incidental dialogue of supporting characters.

Future Boy Conan (*Mirai Shonen Conan*) ran for 28 episodes, April 4–October 31, 1978, on NHK, and was directed by Hayao Miyazaki, Isao Takahata, and Keiji Hayakawa, and produced by Nippon Animation. This was a strange choice. There have been many Japanese animated adaptations for TV of American classic children's literature—*Anne of Green Gables, Little Women, Adventures of Huckleberry Finn, Rascal: The Story of a Raccoon, The Yearling, The Call of the Wild, The Story of Helen Keller*, even Paul Gallico's *Manxmouse*—but this was an adaptation of *The Incredible Tide* by Alexander Key, a very minor boys' science-fiction novel by a very minor author from a very minor publisher (Westminster Press, February 1970). What Were They Thinking?

The Incredible Tide is set five years after a cataclysmic war that destroyed the world. The planet was thrown off its axis, the northern and southern polar icecaps have melted, and only the peaks of the tallest mountains remain above the water as isolated islands. Conan, a 17-year-old orphan who has lived alone on his island since the disaster, is rescued/drafted by the New Order, the successors of the fascist power that started the war. He learns that the New Order has established an uneasy trading relationship with High Harbor, where the remnant of the Western powers are building a new nation. The peaceful inhabitants of High Harbor are waiting fatalistically until the militaristic New Order feels strong enough to annex it. Conan will become their new leader who, with God's help (Key was raised by his grandfather, a southern Methodist minister), will save both sides from the giant tsunami that will engulf the new nations.

Co-director Hayao Miyazaki, who has gone on to better things, rewrote the story heavily, but kept the basic plot of two forces on tiny islands that are all that is left of the world. Key's undated story is set in

2021. Both new sides originate in highly organized socialist Industria. The "good" side renounces regimentation and, led by Dr. Lao, escapes after the war to a distant island they name High Harbour to live in a simpler agrarian society. The remainder of Industria is taken over by dictator Lepka, who is searching for High Harbour to conquer it and use Dr. Lao's efficient solar power to rule the world. Conan has become an eleven-year-old semi-mutant with super-powerful feet that permit him to hang from a ledge by his toes, or run up the sides of buildings and along the wings of aircraft in flight; he also has limited telepathy so he can communicate with Lanna (who is distant from Conan throughout most of the novel; Miyazaki makes her a major onstage character). The semi-villainous Commissioner Dyce of Industria is converted into a friendly supporting character. The bullying teenager Orlo of High Harbor, a major antagonist in the novel, is reduced to a minor character, and Conan is given a new boy-pal, Jimsy.

Miyazaki's dynamic direction has made this a fan favorite for over thirty years, with anime fans who have no idea that it is based on an American s-f novel instead of being an original Japanese scenario.

Rascal the Raccoon (*Araiguma Rascal*), an adaptation of Sterling North's *Rascal, a Memoir of a Better Era* (1963), ran for 52 episodes, January 2–December 25, 1977, and was directed by Seiji Endo and Hiroshi Saito (episodes 1–29) and Shigeo Koshi (episodes 30–52), and produced by Nippon Animation

North's memoir of his childhood, raising a pet baby raccoon in rural Wisconsin in the 1910s, was an American bestseller upon its publication. It got, or was nominated for, several Young Adult literary awards, and was filmed as a live-action feature by Disney in 1969. North's account of how the almost-angelic Rascal brought the estranged young North and his father back together must have seemed a natural for a Japanese children's TV show. Also, North's episodic book was very easy to break down into separate TV episodes. Finally, it had the allure of a cute exotic animal unknown in Japan, almost but not quite like the Japanese tanuki/raccoon dog.

Unfortunately, *Rascal the Raccoon* was so popular with Japanese children that it became responsible for the importation of thousands of North American raccoon cubs into Japan as pets. Enough of them were released into the wild after they grew into non-cute adults (North's book similarly ends with his releasing Rascal when the raccoon grows up and becomes destructive) to create a serious imported-alien-wildlife problem today. The PBS nature film *Raccoon Nation*, broadcast on February 8, 2012, documents how the baby raccoons brought into Japan during the *Rascal* craze of 1977, and released when they grew up, had increased without predators to become a modern plague in mountainous areas, destroying Shinto and Buddhist shrines up to a thousand years old. Despite this, *Rascal the Raccoon* remains so popular in Japan after almost forty years that Nippon Animation still maintains a *Rascal* website where *Rascal* merchandise may be bought. A report on the Tokyo Anime Fair 2013 in March says, "...a lot of lovely *Rascal* merchandise new for 2013: plushies, pens, bags,...". Edgerton, Wisconsin, which has maintained North's late 19th-century/early 20th-century boyhood home as a local-boy-makes-good museum, has recorded Japanese tourists coming to see Rascal's real home.

Nippon Animation has been vigorous in making YouTube remove clips of *Rascal the Raccoon*, and Disney's movie contract does not allow any other cinematic version of *Rascal* to be shown in America; hence, the TV cartoon, popular worldwide, has never been shown in America. Dailymotion has videos of the German dub subtitled in Spanish, but without the original Japanese theme or background music, it's just not the same.

Tomb of Dracula (*Yami no Teio: Kyuketsuki Dracula; Lord of Darkness: the Vampire Dracula*), a 95-minute TV movie (81 minutes plus commercials) was broadcast August 19, 1980, and directed by Minoru Okazaki and Akinori Nagaoka for Toei Animation as a condensed adaptation of most of the 1972-1979 70-issue *Tomb of Dracula* Marvel comic book. Marvel and Toei Animation were considering several co-productions in the late 1970s. Nothing came of the proposed Marvel comic-book adaptations of Toei properties, but Toei made a live-action *Spider-Man* TV serial (with a plot more imitative of Japanese super-sentai shows similar to those Americanized as the *Mighty Morphin' Power Rangers* ; see my discussion of *Spider-Man* in a previous chapter, "Super Sentai Shows"), and animated TV movies of Marvel's *Tomb of Dracula* and *Monster of Frankenstein* comic books.

Tomb of Dracula was a success in two respects: its faithfulness to Gene Colan's comic-book artwork, and a lovely symphonic score featuring a harpsichord by Seiji Yokoyama. Otherwise, it was cringeworthy bad. The animation was so limited that the standard put-down of a limited animated production being little more than a fast-changing slide show springs to mind. Its worst aspect was actually its faithfulness to the first 52 or 53 issues of the comic book, instead of picking one of the comic book's many story arcs and developing it in some depth. The movie switched from one comic-book plot to another with confusing speed, apparently adding and dropping supporting characters at random.

An added insult was its release in America as a direct-to-video animated movie, titled *Dracula: Sovereign of the Damned*, with a laughably bad dub by Harmony Gold Ltd.—overly melodramatic dialogue read by voice actors in bored or hoked-up voices.

Anime fans got bad video copies of the Japanese TV broadcast in late 1980 or early 1981, just as Marvel's management was denying it existed. This was partly to explain to fans why the company was not selling it, but more to fend off demands from the comic's creators for royalties. I have a personal story here. One evening I got a telephone call from Marv Wolfman, the regular writer of the comic for most of its 70 issues. He and his friend Len Wein had been discussing the persistent rumors that *Tomb of Dracula* had been animated in Japan, despite Marvel management's denial, and somebody had just given them my name as a fan of Japanese animation who might know whether this was so. When I answered that I actually had a copy of it on video, Wolfman pleaded with me to drop everything and drive over to his house so they could make a copy of it. I never found out directly what happened next, but it is public knowledge that Marvel fired Wolfman rather than give him any royalties (more for Wolfman's creation of Blade, Vampire Hunter, a supporting character in the comic book whom Marvel had licensed to be featured in an original live-action movie trilogy, than for *Tomb of Dracula* itself).

The Horrors of World War II

Ever since Japan's surrender at the end of World War II, the Japanese have been conflicted about the amount of blame they bear for the war. The Japanese military, of course; nobody has anything good to say about the military-controlled government that got them into a losing war. But the people?

Starting in 1983, there have been several animated accounts of the horrific events of 1945, from the privations of the civilians who were literally starving, to the American military's fire-bombing of several cities, culminating in the nuclear bombings of Hiroshima and Nagasaki. The stories are all told from the viewpoint of helpless civilians, usually children. From 1988 to 1991, there was an annual summer movie, directed by Seiji Arihara and animated by Mushi Productions for release through the Nikkatsu theater chain as a Nikkatsu Children's Movie. The genre has slowed since then, but not died out.

Here is a list of them.

Barefoot Gen (*Hadashi no Gen*) is the thinly-fictionalized autobiography of producer Keiji Nakazawa (1939–2012), a cartoonist who, as a six-year-old boy, lived through the atomic bombing of Hiroshima, witnessing his father and younger brother dying, crying for help, in the flaming rubble of their home. Nakazawa spent his life telling his wartime experiences through manga and animation. Nakazawa focused less blame on the American military for the bomb than on the Japanese military who started the war, and on the civilians who ignored his calls for help for himself, his badly-injured mother, and his dying little sister, shrugging him off with the excuse that "we've got troubles of our own".

Theatrical release: July 21, 1983 (85 minutes), directed by Mori Masaki, with animation by Gen Productions and Studio Madhouse.

Its sequel, **Barefoot Gen 2** (*Hadashi no Gen 2*), continued Gen's/Keiji Nakazawa's story, adapted from volume 2 of his manga, *Barefoot Gen: Out of the Ashes*, and is set in 1948. Life is more positive, thanks to massive food donations by the American occupation forces (whom Gen hates), but Hiroshima is only beginning to rebuild and Gen and his mother have a very difficult time. Gen begins to mix his hard life with the play of a normal nine-year-old. But the first long-term effect of the bomb's radiation on the survivors are seen, including Gen's mother's impending death from cancer.

Theatrical release: June 14, 1986 (86 minutes), directed again by Mori Masaki, with animation by Gen Productions and Studio Madhouse.

The two *Barefoot Gen* movies were basically work-for-hire productions by Studio Madhouse for Gen Productions, Nakazawa's company that was funded mostly by donations from anti-war activists. In addition to the two Gen movies, Nakazawa and Gen Productions made **Summer with Kuro** (*Kuro ga ita natsu*), a 67 minute theatrical feature released June 4, 1990, and directed by Takeshi Shirato, with animation by RCC Chugaku Broadcasting. It is the fictional story of Kuro (Blackie), a cute kitten who lives through the nuclear destruction of Hiroshima.

Grave of the Fireflies (*Hotaru no Haka*), based on a semibiographical novel by Akiyuki Nosaka, tells the story, in flashback after his death, of Seita, a fourteen-year-old boy. He and his little sister Setsuko survive the March 16-17, 1945, firebombing that destroys Kobe and kills their mother. Left orphaned, the two children slowly starve to death amidst the chaos of Japanese society in the last months of the war.

A commercial failure because it is so depressing (since it is narrated by a young ghost, the audience knows from the beginning that it will have an unhappy ending), *Grave of the Fireflies* received almost unanimous rave reviews from critics, in Japan upon its theatrical release and in America upon its video release. Roger Ebert praised it in 2000 as one of the most beautiful anti-war films ever made. "*Grave of the Fireflies* is an emotional experience so powerful that it forces a rethinking of animation. [...] *Grave of the Fireflies* is a powerful dramatic film that happens to be animated, and I know what the critic Ernest Rister means when he compares it to *Schindler's List* and says, 'It is the most profoundly human animated film I've ever seen.'"

> *Theatrical release: April 16, 1988, directed by Isao Takahata, with animation by Studio Ghibli.*

Girls in Summer Clothes (*Natsufuku no Shojo-tachi*), was broadcast on August 7, 1988, the 43rd anniversary of the Hiroshima nuclear bomb blast. In April 1945, the second- and third-year students of a girls' school in Hiroshima are drafted for war work, leaving the 220 first-year girls almost alone. They become close friends. One of them, Yoko Moriwaki, keeps a diary, and much of the anime is based on the diary entries. The diary ends abruptly on August 7, 1945. None of the girls survive the nuclear blast.

> *TV special: August 7, 1988 (34 minutes plus 16 minutes of commercial), directed by Toshio Hirata and Yoshiyuki Momose, with animation by Studio Madhouse.*

Raining Fire (*Hi no Ame ga Furu*), is an anime adaptation of a book containing eye-witness accounts of the fire-bombing of Fukuoka on June 19, 1945, presented as the observations of two children.

> *Theatrical release: September 15, 1988 (80 minutes), directed by Seiji Arihara, with animation by Mushi Productions.*

Kayoko's Diary (*Ushiro no Shomen Daare*; *The Front of the Back*), based on the autobiography of Kayoko Ebina, tells the story of Kayoko, a little girl just starting first grade in Tokyo in 1940. As the war continues and she grows older, she goes from "fun" patriotic efforts such as singing martial songs in school and donating her plastic dolly to make explosives, to growing desperate privation as all food and resources are sent to the military. She is sent to the countryside to escape the American bombing of her city. She can see the distant lights of Tokyo until the night of March 10, 1945, when Tokyo is fire-bombed; after that, the city is dark. When she returns as the war ends, her neighborhood has been leveled and her family is dead.

> *Theatrical release: September 3, 1991 (90 minutes), directed by Seiji Arihara, with animation by Mushi Productions.*

Rail of the Star (*O-Hoshisama no Rail*) tells the true story of Chitose (Chiko) Kobayashi, who grew up as a little girl in Japanese-occupied Pyongyang, Korea, in the late 1930s and early 1940s. As she grew older, her family life deteriorated with Japan's defeats in the war, and she realized the hatred of the Koreans toward their Japanese masters. With Japan's surrender in 1945, the Kobayashis are thrown out of their upper-class home by the Koreans (it had been seized from a Korean in the first place for Japanese settlers to live in). When it is announced that Pyongyang will fall into the U.S.S.R. occupation zone, Chiko's father decides to take the family on a risky migration by foot at night to U.S.-occupied South Korea, following the North Star.

Yes, everyone knows that "The Starlight Railway" would be a better translation, but the Japanese rights-holder insisted upon a more-or-less literal translation. A literal translation would be "Divine Star of Rail".
TV special: July 10, 1993 (79 minutes), directed by Satoru Namekawa and Toshio Hirata, with animation by Studio Madhouse.

The Angelus Bells (*Nagasaki 1945: Angelus no Kane*) tells the story of idealistic young Dr. Akizuki who is assigned to run a tuberculous hospital near a closed Christian theological seminary on the outskirts of Nagasaki. He and his devoted staff are overwhelmed with critically injured and dying patients after the second atomic bomb is dropped on August 9, 1945.
Theatrical release: September 9, 2005 (80 minutes), directed by Seiji Arihara, with animation by Mushi Productions.

To close, it should be noted that the Japanese have produced two feature-length adaptations of *The Diary of Anne Frank* (the actual title of the book is *The Diary of a Young Girl*).

- *Anne no Nikki: Anne Frank Monogatori* (*The Diary of Anne Frank: Anne Frank's Story*), a two-hour TV special movie (1 hour and 25 minutes without commercials) by Nippon Animation that aired on September 28, 1979.

- *Anne no Nikki*, a 102-minute theatrical feature by Studio Madhouse, released on August 19, 1995.

The 1979 semi-realistic TV movie, directed by Eiji Okabe, features naturalistic designs for the actual story, which is broken up by Anne's Picasso-like surrealistic dream sequences. The more realistic, better animated, but less imaginative 1995 theatrical feature, directed by Akinori Nagaoka, is mostly notable for its music by Michael Nyman. The soundtrack album contains 19 tracks.

To some extent, these two features balanced all of the animation showing Japanese children as the innocent victims of war. War is cruel to the civilians of all nations.

Debunking the Myths

Crusader Rabbit and Walt Disney

How much of what everyone "knows" about animation history is wrong? For example...

MYTH: The first TV cartoon was *Crusader Rabbit*, in 1949. And Crusader always fought the villainous Dudley Nightshade.

That's what IMDb seems to say, all right. Also TV.com, the TV IV, the Museum of Broadcast Communications, TV Tropes, Skooldays, Inner Toob, and other online sites of "nostalgia" information about the early days of television. Other sites such as Wikipedia, the Archive of American Television, Digital Media FX, WikiFur, and Animation World Media give the correct date of August 1, 1950. Still others such as IMDb list both dates in different parts of their articles, or avoid giving any date at all in their information about *Crusader Rabbit*.

Thorough researchers, such as myself through the pages of *TV Guide* for 1949 and 1950, give the correct date as August 1, 1950. *Crusader Rabbit* started production in early 1949, and producer Jerry Fairbanks promoted it furiously all through 1949 and 1950 in press releases and trade magazine advertisements as being available for TV syndication. But the first actual sale and broadcast was to KNBH in Los Angeles beginning August 1, 1950.

Where did the 1949 date, sometimes even specified as September 1, 1949, come from? Possibly from a dated magazine article or advertisement. Also, Fairbanks' promotion may have included giving the first one or two finished episodes to TV children's programs during 1949, to let them be seen. *Crusader Rabbit* was certainly in production during 1949. Nevertheless, the contracted first 130 episodes were not finished until the series had definitely been sold, to begin airing on August 1, 1950. The record has always been clear on this. The final 65 episodes were added during 1951.

As to whether Cru's adversary was always Dudley Nightshade, that was in the color series only. When producer Shull Bonsall took over directors

Alex Anderson's & Jay Ward's 1949–51 195-episode black-and-white series and decided to make the color sequels in 1957, he got the brainstorm of combining all of Cru's villains into one. He was openly inspired by *Time for Beany*'s Dishonest John, since Bonsall claimed that Dudley Nightshade predated Dishonest John and was the first TV cartoon villain! (True only if you quibble that D.J. was a hand puppet at first, not a cartoon. *Time for Beany* first appeared on Los Angeles local TV on February 28, 1949, and went national the next year.) Cru's "crusades" each had a different villain at first. The first, "Crusader vs. the State of Texas" (15 episodes), was technically an adversary, not a villain. Frank Sawbuck was a big game hunter type who had been hired by the Texas government to rid Texas of jackrabbits, because they were eating all the carrots that Texan sharpshooters needed for their keen vision. Cru persuaded the rabbits to switch from carrots to tastier creampuffs, and everybody was happy.

But the others were genuine villains:

- In Crusade #2, "Crusader vs. the Pirates" (20 episodes), it was Black Bilge and his pirates.
- In #3, "Crusader and the Rajah of Rinsewater" (20 episodes), the villain was Dudley Nightshade, a crooked royal advisor.
- In #4, "Crusader and the Schmohawk Indians" (15 episodes), Cru and the Indians were pitted against Chicago gangster-type Babyface Barracuda and his mob.
- In #5, "Crusader and the Great Horse Mystery" (20 episodes), the villain was glue magnate Gaston Glub, who was kidnapping all the racehorses in Kentucky to steal their hooves to make Glub's Glue.
- In #6, "Crusader and the Circus" (10 episodes), Cru and Rags were pitted against a crooked circus ringmaster, Whetstone Whiplash, and his henchman, the dishonest circus strongman, Bilious Greene.
- In #7, "Crusader in the Tenth Century" (30 episodes), a time-travel adventure, Cru and Rags go back a thousand years to confront the medieval Blaggard brothers (Blackheart, Brimstone, and Bigot) and their two-headed dragon, Arson and Sterno.
- In #8, "Crusader and the Mad Hollywood Scientist" (15 episodes), Cru and Rags save Hollywood from mad scientist Belfrey Q. Batts who aimed to uglify all of the handsome actors, and at one point turned Rags into a flightless vulture.

At that point, Alex Anderson & Jay Ward became concerned that Crusader Rabbit and Rags the Tiger (Ragland T. Tiger) were their only recurring characters. They decided that they should have a larger regular cast. So with Crusade #9, "Crusader and the Leprechauns" (25 episodes), they gave Cru & Rags a tagalong friend, Garfield Groundhog, and they started recycling their villains. #9 featured Dudley Nightshade, who was fleecing the leprechauns of Ireland, and #10, "Crusader and the Showboat" (25 episodes), had the return of Whetstone Whiplash, who had become a crooked Mississippi riverboat captain with Bilious Greene as his first mate.

Only Dudley Nightshade and Whetstone Whiplash really looked alike. Both were caricatures of the stereotyped 19th-century melodrama villain: tall and lean, dressed all in black with a cape that he flourished, and a thin, black moustache that he twirled. Bonsall took advantage of the fact that by 1959, when he released the color series, nobody clearly remembered the old 1949–51 episodes. Even though he offered both series for sale, TV stations wanted only the color episodes with better animation. So the public bought his story that Cru's nemesis was always Dudley Nightshade in different disguises. And in the color episodes, he was.

Actually, Bonsall used the character design of Whetstone Whiplash with Dudley's name, because Whetstone looked meaner. The original Dudley *might* hesitate to steal candy from a baby. There was no doubt that Whetstone would not hesitate.

MYTH: Out of public sight, the real Walt Disney was a bitter, foul-mouthed bigot who refused to hire Jews or blacks.

This is a myth that just should not exist. Even if it did not pop up until after Disney was dead and no longer around to deny it, there are plenty of veteran Disney employees who knew Walt personally; not only can they deny the myth, they have! Often! But it continues to be perpetuated, just like the one that Walt has had his body frozen in cryogenic suspension and entombed beneath Disneyland's Pirates of the Caribbean attraction, to be thawed out when medical science catches up with the cancer that killed him. (Walt Disney died of a heart attack just after an operation for an incurable cancer, probably as the result of post-operative stress. His body was cremated, and the ashes buried at Forest Lawn Memorial Park Cemetery.)

Walt did use the swear words that almost any adult male frequently uses, and he may have used some of the racially prejudicial terms like "nigger" and "to jew down" that were common before about the 1950s. But Floyd Norman, an African-American active in anti-prejudice organizations, was hired by the Disney studio in the 1950s and often saw and worked directly with Disney before his death. Norman, who was recognized by the Company in 2007 as a Disney Legend, has said emphatically that Disney showed no sign of being racist or having any objection to hiring black employees.

As for Jews, one of Disney's earliest animators was Isadore "Friz" Freleng. Freleng did not work for Disney in Kansas City, but he grew up there and he knew several of Disney's animators. When Walt moved to Hollywood, he invited Freleng to join his studio. Freleng worked with Disney on *Oswald, the Lucky Rabbit* for several months in 1927. Freleng next animated for Charles Mintz, who took the Oswald cartoons away from Disney in 1928, for a year until Universal took the Oswald cartoons away from him, and Mintz closed his studio. Most of Mintz's animators ended up working for Leon Schlesinger making Warner Bros. cartoons. There is a story that when Bob Clampett made the 1944 *Russian Rhapsody* short, with caricatures of all the Schlesinger staff as the gremlins who are wrecking Adolf Hitler's airplane in mid-air, WB got a complaint about a gross drawing of a Jew, looking just like a Nazi caricature of a big-nosed Jew among the other self-caricatures. That was "Friz" Freleng, who really did look like an exaggerated parody of a Jew. He was just as obviously Jewish when he was working directly under Disney, and openly professed his religion.

Another prominent Jew at Disney was Art Babbitt, who defined the look of Goofy in the 1930s short cartoons. Disney came to personally hate Babbitt, but not because he was Jewish; it was because he was a leader of the anti-Disney studio strike in 1941. Disney later publicly accused Babbitt of "probably" being a Communist, but made no complaints about his Jewishness. During the 1950s, Disney was openly friendly with producer Samuel Goldwyn, who made no secret of the fact that he was a Polish Jew named Schmuel Gelbfisz when he came to America. Michael Labrie, the director of collections at the Walt Disney Family Museum in San Francisco, has said, "Walt was named 'Man of the Year' in 1955 by the B'nai B'rith chapter of Beverly Hills, and in 1958 won an award from Hadassah, the Women's Zionist Organization of America. I'm convinced they would never have given those honors to an anti-Semite."

But not only do the rumors of Disney's poisonous anti-Semitism persist, they grow more widespread and more blatant. There are the three biographies filled with anti-Disney hate that has been disproven, but they are cited again and again as proof: *Disney's World: A Biography* (Stein & Day, 1983) and *The Real Walt Disney* (HarperCollins, April 1986), both by Leonard Mosley; and *Walt Disney: Hollywood's Dark Prince*, by Marc Eliot (Birch Lane Press, July 1993). There are the anti-Disney jokes on *Family Guy* ("Are the Jews gone yet?"), *Robot Chicken*, and *Saturday Night Live* (Walt Disney is asked how he thawed out early. "Science says global warming, but I can't help thinking it has something to do with Jews!")

In June 1934, Disney announced to the public his decision to make a feature-length film, *Snow White and the Seven Dwarfs*. The workaholic Disney was showing signs of another nervous breakdown by early 1935 (he had already had one in 1931), and his brother Roy persuaded him to get away from the pressure by taking a family working vacation to Europe that summer. It lasted from mid-June to mid-August. Walt, wife Lillian, brother Roy, and Roy's wife Edna disembarked from the luxury liner *Normandie* in Plymouth on June 12, went to London where they discussed the booking of Disney films with British cinema executives, and then to Paris in early July. They rented a car and drove to Münich where Disney films were playing at a theater, and Roy signed a contract with Baveria Filmkunst Gmbh. to take over the distribution of Disney films in Germany. Their itinerary shows that they were in Münich from July 7 to 9. They next drove to Milan and Venice, where the 3rd International Film Festival was showing. Disney's *The Band Concert* received an award. Then to Rome, where the Disneys were wined and dined by the Minister of Propaganda, Count Galeazzo Ciano. A gala evening was held for Disney at the Italian premiere of an American movie. After a couple of similar publicity events, the Disneys went on to Naples and Capri, then returned to America in the Italian ocean liner *Rex* in mid-August.

An enjoyable vacation, and well-documented. Nobody questioned it for over sixty years. Then, in the 2000s, the anti-Disney rumor mill began to claim that Disney had snuck away while they were in Münich and driven to Berchtesgaden to see Adolf Hitler! Reportedly, the two men congratulated each other on their anti-Semitism. This was even built up into a play, *Disney in Deutschland*, by John J. Powers, which had at least two productions by the Wunderland Theatre Group in San Francisco, first at the Next Stage Theatre on June 8-24, 2007, and then at the Garage Playhouse beginning January 31, 2008. The first production was reviewed by animation fan Harry McCracken:

> The piece takes place in 1935 at Hitler's Berchtesgaden mountain home, with a set that sports such authentic decorations as a "gramophone" with an LCD display and a book with a bar code on the jacket. Hitler (John Strain) is there with Leni Riefenstahl (Donna K. Moore)—they can't keep their hands off each other, which, as far as I know, is an alternate-reality touch in itself—and they're anticipating Disney's visit.
>
> They're quite excited about it: "Disney's our mensch!," burbles Adolf. Leni, however, does point out that "his films were banned here for years because some animal—a duck, I think—ridiculed the Kaiser."
>
> Walt arrives; as played by Brendan Scoggin, he looks and behaves more like Hal "The Great Gildersleeve" Peary than the Disney we know.

"Goebbels tells me that you make pictures for children," comments Hitler by way of conversation.

"Herr Hitler, I don't know if you know this, but you have quite a following in America," says Walt genially, mentioning that he's attended Nazi rallies in Los Angeles. He spews hatred at Hollywood rivals like "that damned Jew at Universal." And boasts that he manages to avoid interaction with the Jews because "we create, produce, and distribute—we do everything ourselves!" (Apparently, Buena Vista existed in 1935; we just didn't know it.)

Suddenly inspired to play storyman, Adolf attempts to convince Walt to make a cartoon based on a Brothers Grimm tale called "The Jew and the Thornbush," but Walt seems skeptical of its potential. Even so, they're kindred spirits, and Walt recognizes it: "Herr Hitler, we're doing the same thing, but in different ways."

And then they really bond when Walt confides in Adolf that he remains tormented by how Elias stripped him naked and beat him as a child; a compassionate Adolf tells Walt that his father loved him even so.

All along, both Walt and Adolf have been admiring a large scale model of Germania, Hitler's planned renewal project for Berlin. Walt loves it, seeing it as a place with interesting buildings, attractions, and things for families to do together. You almost expect him to start talking about E tickets and churros.

Finally, Walt gets to the point of his visit: He wants Adolf to allow the distribution of Disney cartoons in Germany. Adolf agrees, on one condition: that if anything happens to him, Walt will see to it that Germania is built in some form or fashion. We see an image of Germany's fairytale-like Neuschwanstein castle, famous for inspiring the Disneyland castle, projected behind them. The performance ends.

The record has always been clear that *Crusader Rabbit* did not begin TV syndication until August 1950, and that Walt Disney, before his death in 1966, was never an anti-Semitic, pro-Nazi bigot. But if anything seems certain, it is that it does not matter how often the myths are disproven. Informational sites will continue to state that *Crusader Rabbit* was released in 1949, and popular "everybody knows" information about Walt Disney will portray him as anti-black and a Jew-hater. Now it's even in opera! Philip Glass' *The Perfect American*, which debuted in Madrid's Teatro Real in January 2013, features Disney just before his death, having a surrealistic conversation with the audioanimatronic Abraham Lincoln that he built for Disneyland. Lincoln espouses the liberalism of the Emancipation Proclamation, while Disney responds with questions that strongly hint at a racist bias. "Martin Luther King, Eldridge Cleaver, is that what you wanted? Doesn't that go too far even for you, Mr. President? The black people's march in Washington; would you really agree with that?"

Like the classic Walt Disney himself, the legends are larger than life, and they will continue to grow.

Leon Schlesinger/Eddie Selzer and Balto

In the last chapter, I asked "How much of what everyone 'knows' about animation history is wrong?" Here are two more widespread animation myths.

MYTH: The Warner Bros. cartoons were so great because studio bosses Leon Schlesinger and Eddie Selzer took no interest in them, and had no idea what their animators were turning out.

This myth is attributable directly to WB director Chuck Jones. He said so. He should know, shouldn't he?

Leon Schlesinger (1884–1949) worked in East Coast movie theaters in his youth, and later moved to "Hollywood" where most of the cinema industry was located. In 1919, he founded Pacific Title & Art Studio in Burbank, to make title cards for silent movies. In 1930, he was contacted by Rudolph Ising and Hugh Harmon from a team of movie animators who had been making the *Oswald, the Lucky Rabbit* cartoons for producer Charles Mintz, who sold them to Universal Pictures. (Mintz had earlier hired the animators away from Walt Disney, who had created Oswald for Universal.) Universal had just fired Mintz and taken over producing the Oswald cartoons with its own studio, headed by Walter Lantz. Mintz had closed his studio and let all his animators go. Instead of dispersing, Ising and Harmon persuaded them to stay together long enough to see if they could sell their services as a complete animation studio to someone else. Ising and Harmon offered themselves and their fellow animators to Pacific Title & Art. Schlesinger, who could see the disappearance of movie title cards with the introduction of sound films, in turn offered the services of an animation studio to Warner Bros., the last major motion picture producer that did not have a cartoon department. WB hired him, and Schlesinger hired Ising and Harmon and the former Mintz animators as Leon Schlesinger Studios. In 1934, after a dispute with Ising and Harmon, the two left Schlesinger, taking their cartoon star Bosko with them. Schlesinger quickly hired back most of the other animators, plus some from other studios, and arranged with WB to set up his own studio on the WB lot, later dubbed "Termite Terrace" by the animators. (Schlesinger sold Pacific Title & Art Studio in 1935 to concentrate on his animation studio. PT&A is still in business as a general post-production house for the movie and TV industries.)

Schlesinger's own offices were not in the ramshackle animation building, which helped to create a feeling of separation between the animators and management. The animators have told similar stories about Schlesinger briefly looking in upon them every so often, and saying approximately, "How are you boys doing? Is everything okay? Well, keep up the good work." The plump Schlesinger, who wore an obvious toupee, reeked of cologne, and dressed nattily in a white suit, made no secret that he considered himself above his working-man animators. He owned a yacht, often spent all day at the horse races, and commented aloud about the Termite Terrace workshop, "I wouldn't work in a shithole like this." This increased the animators' willingness to make fun of him.

But it was good-natured fun. Rather than not caring about the animators except for the money that their cartoons brought in, most of the animators agreed that Schlesinger kept a close eye on his studio and deliberately gave them maximum creative freedom. His attitude, openly expressed, was, "I pay you boys to make funny cartoons. As long as the public likes your work and you stay within budget, you can do whatever you think will bring in the laughs." Schlesinger jovially agreed not only to let his animators make Christmas gag reels in 1939 and 1940, he participated in them. Schlesinger also agreed to star in a combination live-action/animated short directed by "Friz" Freleng, *You Ought to Be in Pictures* (May 1940), playing himself as the head of his studio with Porky Pig and Daffy Duck (animated) unhappy with their contracts. Other Schlesinger employees also appear in *You Ought to Be in Pictures*, including writer Michael Maltese as a WB studio guard, and Henry Binder, Schlesinger's executive assistant, as a stagehand.

After Ising and Harmon left, it was Schlesinger who put Friz Freleng in charge of his studio, and hired such animators as Tex Avery, Bob Clampett, Frank Tashlin, and Chuck Jones, and voice artist Mel Blanc and musician Carl Stalling. According to animation historians, it was Schlesinger who made the final decision to name Bugs Bunny. The character had already become a favorite at the studio among the animators, and was unofficially known as "Bugs" from being labeled as "Bugs' Bunny" on a model sheet for Ben "Bugs" Hardaway, the first director to use him. In 1940 Tex Avery directed *A Wild Hare*, the first cartoon where the rabbit would have to have a name. Avery called him Jack Rabbit. (Mel Blanc said it was Happy Rabbit.) The rest of the cartoon's animators wanted to make the Bugs Bunny name official. The argument grew so heated that both sides took it to Schlesinger to decide. Schlesinger said

Bugs Bunny, definitely. It was already in use by most of the animators, it was a more striking name than the generic Jack Rabbit, and it fit the smart-aleck personality of the rabbit. The disappointed Avery quit and went to MGM. It was also Schlesinger who named Bob Clampett's notorious *Coal Black and de Sebben Dwarfs*. Clampett intended to name it *So White and de Sebben Dwarfs*, but Schlesinger worried that that was too close to Disney's original.

Tom Sito, a veteran animator and animation historian, and president of the Motion Picture Screen Cartoonist's Local 839 (animation's professional labor union) from 1992 to 2001, commented on a 2008 story on the Cartoon Brew website about Schlesinger's obituary:

> Many Termite Terrace vets who disparaged Leon's leadership, all admit what Leon was best at was keeping the meddling suits from the main lot from annoying the artists with their "creative" opinions. We could use a lot more Leon Schlesingers today. Leon also was a champion of his animation unit and once complained to the Academy that Disney won the short film Oscar too many times.

More pertinently, was Daffy's and Sylvester's juicy lisp copied from Leon Schlesinger's, and was Schlesinger ignorant of this? Maybe, maybe not. Besides Jones in *Chuck Amuck*, cartoon writer and gag man Michael Maltese is quoted in Joe Adamson's *Tex Avery: King of Cartoons* (Popular Library, October 1975) as saying that Schlesinger lisped "a little bit":

> But we were not hampered by any front office interference, because Leon Schlesinger had brains enough to keep the hell away and go aboard his yacht. He used to lithp a little bit and he'd say, "I'm goin' on my yachtht." He'd say, "Whatth cookin', brainth? Anything new in the Thtory Department?" He came back from Mexico once, he had huarachas on, he said, "Whaddya think of these Mexican cucarachas? Very comfortable on the feet." He said, "Disney can make the chicken salad, I wanna make chicken shit." He said, "I'll make money." (pp. 125-126)

Blanc might have based his lisp for the duck's and the cat's speech on Schlesinger's, and exaggerated it to such an extent that Schlesinger did not recognize it as based on his own lisp—or even if he did, he may have recognized that Blanc exaggerated it so outrageously that it was funny. Schlesinger has shown that he could go along with a gag. Basically, by the time *Chuck Amuck: The Life and Times of an Animated Cartoonist* (Farrar, Straus & Giroux, November 1989) was published, Schlesinger was long dead, Clampett was recently dead, and most people didn't care. Jones' story was too good not to repeat. The scenes of Schlesinger in *You Ought to Be in Pictures* and the 1939 & 1940 gag reels, where Schlesinger's real voice is heard, although very brief, do not hint of any lisp on the sound track; though arguably, Schlesinger could have deliberately concentrated on not lisping since he knew that he was talking on camera.

In 1944, Schlesinger sold his animation studio to Warner Bros. and retired. WB officially made the studio its cartoon department, and assigned Edward Selzer (1893-1970) to replace Schlesinger. Selzer, whom everyone agreed was more humorless and formal than Schlesinger, deliberately continued Schlesinger's policy of giving the animators creative freedom as long as they stayed within the increasingly smaller budgets.

Jim Korkis wrote in his "Animation Anecdotes" column (#107), posted April 26, 2013, on the Cartoon Research website:

> Animation legend Chuck Jones was always fond of telling the story of his meeting with Jack and Harry Warner of Warner Brothers Studio. "Friz Freleng and I had a meeting with the two of them. We were taken to the private executive dining room. Jack looked over at us and said, with a mouthful of food, 'You know, I don't even know where our animation studio is.' Harry nodded and said, 'The only thing I know about our cartoon studio is that's where we make Mickey Mouse.' They didn't realize we didn't make Mickey Mouse. When they finally found out, they closed the studio."

Ha ha; very funny! As for being true…. Well, all of the biographies of Jack Warner do agree that he ruthlessly concentrated on the studio's live-action features only, and dismissed the cartoons as worth making only because theater-owners wanted them as part of a complete theatrical package. The WB facilities were huge, and in 1953 the cartoon department was at WB's Sunset Boulevard lot, not the main Burbank lot; so maybe Harry and Jack Warner didn't know exactly where it was. But Jack kept track of whether the cartoons stayed profitable or not, and it was Eddie Selzer's job to see to it that they did.

(On the other hand, one of Harry Warner's other well-known comments, in 1927, was, "Who the hell wants to hear actors talk?", in response to Sam Warner's support for making *The Jazz Singer* a talkie. Fortunately for the world, Sam Warner won that argument—and died the day before the movie's premiere.)

What Jones did say, on page 89 of his *Chuck Amuck* autobiography, was, "Friz Freleng contends that the Warner brothers implicitly believed we made Mickey Mouse, until 1963—when, shocked to discover that we did not, they shut the studio."

Oh, so it's Friz Freleng's story now. By 1963, Harry Warner was dead—he died in 1958—so it was Jack's decision alone to close the animation unit. The reason given by the studio was the increasing production costs of animation, plus falling orders from theater-owners who by the 1960s felt that audiences no longer demanded a cartoon with their feature. That is a more believable reason than that Jack Warner had just found out that WB did not make the Mickey Mouse cartoons.

Two stories do seem verified to Selzer's discredit. In one, Selzer orders Freleng not to team up Tweety with Sylvester. Wikipedia says:

> Some historians also claim that Friz Freleng nearly resigned after butting heads with Selzer, who did not think that pairing Sylvester the cat and Tweety was a viable decision. The argument reached its crux when Freleng reportedly placed his drawing pencil on Selzer's desk, furiously telling Selzer that if he knew so much about animation, he should do the work instead. Selzer backed off the issue and apologized to Freleng that evening.

According to the other story, after director Robert McKimson made the first cartoon featuring the Tasmanian Devil, *Devil May Hare*, in 1954, Selzer ordered him not to made any more because he was afraid that audiences would dislike the ferocious Taz. It was not until Jack Warner personally told Selzer that the Devil was getting "boxes and boxes" of fan mail, and should reappear in the cartoons as soon as possible, that Selzer greenlit Taz's further appearances.

And those two are *not* among Chuck Jones' stories. Jack Warner does not look so ignorant of WB's animation there, as long as it pertained to the studio's overall income.

One story that Jones does tell about Eddie Selzer in *Chuck Amuck* is, on page 93:

> He once appeared in the doorway of our story room while Mike Maltese and I were grappling with a new story idea. Suddenly a furious dwarf stood in the doorway: "I don't want any gags about bullfights, bullfights aren't funny!" Exactly the words he had used to Friz Freleng about never using camels. Out of that dictum came Sahara Hare, one of the funniest cartoons ever made, with the funniest camel ever made.
>
> Having issued his angry edict, Eddie stormed back to his office. Mike and I eyed one another in silent wonderment. "We've been missing something," Mike said. "I never knew there was anything funny about bullfighting until now. But Eddie's judgment is impeccable. He's never been right yet." "God moves in wondrous ways, his story ideas to beget," I replied.
>
> Result: *Bully for Bugs*, one of the best Bugs Bunny cartoons our unit ever produced.

Now, let's see. Eddie Selzer, their boss and an angry man with no sense of humor, had just ordered them to never make a cartoon about bullfighting, and had previously issued a similar order about camels.

Both times, his animators had immediately disobeyed his orders. Are we to believe that, if this had happened at another studio, Walt Disney's maybe, that the boss would not have instantly fired those employees? Maybe Jones meant this to serve as an example of how little Selzer kept track of what went on in his studio. A cartoon short, from every studio, took months to produce, and when it was completed, everyone—including especially the producer—viewed the finished product. Are we to believe that Selzer remained ignorant of the camel and the bullfighting cartoons all during this time? It is more probable that Selzer was aware of and continued Schlesinger's managerial practice: give the staff complete freedom to be as funny as they can, as long as they stay within budget. Also: WB released *Bully for Bugs* on August 8, 1953. *Sahara Hare* was not released until March 26, 1955. Was Freleng over two years in production of *Sahara Hare*, or was Jones less than accurate in his reminiscing?

MYTH: Balto was the lead sled dog of the team that brought the diphtheria serum to Nome, Alaska, in 1925.

This myth is not particularly animation-related, but it was the basis for three animated features: the *Balto* 1995 theatrical feature by Steven Spielberg's Amblimation studio, and the direct-to-video sequels, *Balto II: Wolf Quest* (2002) and *Balto III: Wings of Change* (2004), both produced by Universal Cartoon Studios. So it seems worth covering here.

It is "true, but". In January 1925, Dr. Curtis Welch, the only doctor in Nome, Alaska, isolated by the winter season, discovered that a diphtheria plague was breaking out. The nearest antitoxin was in Anchorage, almost a thousand miles away. No airplane was available; the sub-zero cold made their engines freeze up. The closest that a train could get was the town of Nenana, 304 miles from Anchorage and still 674 miles away. The only way to transport the serum to Nome in time was by dog sled. The 674-mile journey was made by not one but several Siberian husky sled dog teams. Relay teams were organized by radio from Nome and from Nenana. The two would meet at Nulato, a halfway point, where the Nenana team would hand the serum to the Nome team for the return journey.

The teams from Nenana faced -50°F temperatures that went even lower in blizzard conditions. Several dogs died. The last sledder, Henry Ivanoff, decided to go past Nulato to save the Nome team some time. The Nome team was led by sledder Leonhard Seppala, and his lead dog was Togo, named for the Japanese admiral who had won the 1905 Battle of Tsushima. Seppala was travelling through a storm with a wind chill factor of -85°F. It took him four days to reach the point where Ivanoff was, and he would have passed him in the storm if Ivanoff had not called out. Seppala took the serum and turned back to Nome immediately. (There had been seven deaths when he left, and over twenty more confirmed cases.)

Seppala and Togo travelled back across a frozen sound with ice breaking up. He was met en route by Charlie Olsen, who took the serum but was blown off the trail by the storm and suffered extreme frostbite. Olsen made it to where Gunnar Kaasen's team led by Balto was waiting. Kaasen took the serum the rest of the way to Nome. They did pass through some horrific conditions—visibility was so poor that Kaasen could not see his closest sled dog, and he also developed frostbite—but they were relatively fresh when they pulled into Nome. The waiting press hailed Kaasen and Balto as the team who brought the serum from Nulato, or all the way from Anchorage. Seppala and Togo, who had covered the longest and most dangerous distance, were recovering from extreme exhaustion and frostbite at the time. Togo recovered first, and escaped to hunt reindeer. By the time he returned to his kennel, Kaasen and Balto were on the publicity circuit, being praised by the press, President Coolidge, and the U.S. Senate.

Seppala and Togo got plenty of recognition later on. They toured the U.S., and in New York's Madison Square Garden, Togo was given a gold medal by the Swedish explorer Roald Amundsen. But Balto kept getting the greater publicity. There is a statue of Balto in New York's Central Park, and Cleveland's school children raised enough money to buy him. He lived the rest of his life in the Cleveland Zoo, and is stuffed and mounted today in the Cleveland Museum of Natural History. And there are three animated movies (fantasies, but who cares?), to keep his memory alive.

Balto never had offspring; he had been neutered as a young dog. Togo became so popular as a stud dog that most working huskies in the U.S. today are his descendants. Seppala sold the rest of his team to a dog breeder, so today's American huskies who are not descendants of Togo are likely to be descendants of his teammates.

Chapter 5

加西生学由天谊 复

Indian Animation

When I started to get press releases for Indian animation around 2011, along with plenty of "We're now hiring for our new studio in Bangalore!" (or Hyderabad or Chennai or Pune or wherever) recruiting advertisements, I thought that the Indian animation industry must have started recruiting among the American animation industry—and in a big way, if they're sending stuff to me. I have always been a big animation fan, but I have never considered myself a professional animation technician, even if I have written numerous articles and reviews on it, and worked at Streamline Pictures for a dozen years.

But I have since learned that nobody else whom I know seems to be getting these, which leaves me wondering why people in India are sending me all their advertising? Not that I'm complaining, as long as the advertisements contain lots of colorful graphics and animated trailers (which you can find on YouTube).

Here's an example of one such press release:

> "*Chhota Bheem And The Throne Of Bali* To Hit Theatres Tommorrow" (sic) [May 3]

> With the nationwide release of *Chhota Bheem and The Throne of Bali*, India's animation superstar Chhota Bheem will be seen taking on real life stars from *Bombay Talkies* and *Shootout At Wadala* this Friday. To be released in three languages in over five hundred theatres, this will be one of the largest ever-theatrical releases of an Indian animation film. "With an existing viewership of 40 million children, Chhota Bheem's initial draw would be comparable to the highest paid Bollywood stars. Moreover, children as an audience are more loyal. We are quite certain that Chhota Bheem and *The Throne of Bali* will emerge top release of the week and over time give one of the best box office returns," says Samir Jain, co producer. The film is being released in Hindi, Tamil and Telugu. AlluArvind's Geetha Film Distributors and Yash Raj Films will respectively distribute the film in South and rest of India. This is the second Chhota Bheem film to be released. The previous film, *Chhota Bheem and the Curse of Damyaan*, was released in

May 2012 and drew a collection of Rs. 4.92 crores, which is the highest ever collection for an Indian animation film. "Being our first release, the film was exhibited as a morning show in most theatres. But this time round the distribution, marketing and promotions are on a scale comparable to any large commercial film release," added Jain.

And so on. I won't quote it all. What is most interesting about this e-mail press release is two animated clips, including the feature's trailer.

I have been getting these press releases for long enough that I have had to learn a bit about India in self defense. The double-H is fairly common in Hindi. Chhota means brave; Bheem is a personal name. Chhota Bheem is extremely popular with young children in comic books, toys, TV cartoons, and now theatrical features. There are 22 official languages in India; Hindi on the west coast is the most widespread. India was a British colony until 1947, and the British taught English in the schools across India, so it is usual to use English as a common language for theatrical trailers across India instead of dubbing them into 22 different languages. Indian movies have so many song and dance sequences that you'd think that all Indian movies from comedies to science-fiction thrillers are required by law to be part-musicals. The Hindu religion shows its saints as colored bright blue, the equivalent of Christian saints having glowing halos; ordinary people are not supposed to notice this. A crore is ten million, so 4.92 crore rupees would be Rs. 40,920,000. (An Indian rupee is worth approximately U.S. $0.02 at press time.) The abbreviation for the rupee used to be Rs., but in 2010 the Indian government decided that if the supercurrencies like the U.S. dollar ($), the British pound (£),the Japanese yen (¥), and the European Union's euro (€) had their own symbols, the Indian rupee should follow them. The symbol adopted for the rupee is ₹. But until Indian typewriters and computer keyboards get a ₹ key, people can continue to use Rs.

Some of these Indian animated features have subsequently gotten American limited theatrical releases, like *Arjun: The Warrior Prince* and *Hey Krishna*, usually to qualify for an Oscar; or, in the case of *Delhi Safari*, their backers have given up hoping for a theatrical release and settled for a direct-to-DVD release.

One that has not is *Kamlu...Happy Happy*, a 3D CGI feature about a young talking camel who wants to be able to fly. This was promoted as coming to Indian theaters in May 2012 in English and Hindi, from Krayon Pictures, the same studio that made *Delhi Safari*. Director/producer Govind Nihalani was interviewed on Indian TV; he is apparently a well-known Indian live-action director who had agreed to make *Kamlu...Happy Happy* because he liked the challenge of making an animated movie. "My film is not Tom & Jerry," he said. *Kamlu...Happy Happy* would be feature-length and have a real plot, with a message for children of being true to your dreams and not letting critics discourage you. Since then, nothing. Was *Kamlu...Happy Happy* ever released?

One studio frequently mentioned has been Prana Studios, with offices in Mumbai and Los Angeles. One of its more intriguing movies is *Koochie Koochie Hota Hai*, a 3-D CGI feature starring three anthropomorphized dogs (actually a funny-animal remake of the 1998 Indian live-action musical *Kuch Kuch Hota Hai*) in a time-travel romantic comedy plot. This feature was apparently completed at least three years ago, but for unexplained (presumably legal) reasons its release keeps getting postponed. (It's currently scheduled for release in 2015.) I had assumed that Prana is primarily a studio for Indian animation production, until I learned that it has been producing the direct-to-DVD *Tinker Bell* features as a Disney subcontractor; has produced the forthcoming American releases of *Planes* and *Legends of Oz: Dorothy's Return*; and has just bought the bankrupt Los Angeles Rhythm & Hues VFX studio, the producer of the VFX in *Life of Pi*, for $30,000,000. And yes, Prana is advertising that it is hiring at both its Los Angeles and Mumbai offices.

Over half of the Indian animated features that I get advertising for are based on Hindu mythology, the Hindu equivalent of Bible stories. You would think that these are extremely unlikely to ever get American releases, but one that is currently trying has the American title of *Hey Krishna*. It is being promoted as an adventure fantasy in America; in India, it is a religious film about the first ten years or so of Krishna's life, up to where he fights and kills his evil uncle King Kans. I got a lot of advertising for it when it was titled *Krishna aur Kans* (*Krishna versus Kans*) and about to be released in India in August 2012, in English, Hindi, Tamil, and Telugu. The Indian advertising was much more devout, always referring to him as "Lord Krishna".

Another was Toonz Animation India's *Swami Ayyappan*, released in October 2012, in the Kannada, Malayam, Tamil, and Telugu languages. At least *Hey Krishna* has excellent (if not quite up to Pixar's level) CGI animation. One feature that is especially unlikely to be released in America is Landmark Toonz's *Luv Kush—The Sons of Rama,* which is both overly Hindu religious, and is some of the crappiest theatrical animation that I have ever seen!

To give you a better sense of the amount of Indian animation publicity that I receive, here are some snippets of stories from the September 2013 issue of *Animation Xpress*, the Indian industry online newsletter from which these press releases are taken.

September 2. *Virtual Thought*, a 2'24" CGI student film, wins an award:

> Rahul Punyani's [...] short *Virtual Thought* was screened at ANIFEST INDIA 2013 and [won] the Student Category Award.
>
> *What challenges did you face in the making of the short?*
>
> "The shot in which several particles had to form into a car within few seconds was tricky. It took me around 15 days thinking about how to make this possible. The rendering software crashed while editing this shot. And as I didn't want to compromise with the quality of this movie, I ended up using Cinema 4D software for the same. I used three software for this movie, namely 3D Max Software was used for modeling the characters, After Effects for the composition, and Cinema 4D software for the sequence."

September 4. *Toah's Ark*, not a student film, wins another award:

> Bangalore-based Morph Digital Studio's animation short *Toah's Ark* has won the Planet Water Video Contest [...] in the Animation Category.
>
> AnimationXpress.com [asked] Anirudh Goutham, Director of Morph Digital Studio, about the making *Toah's Ark*.
>
> *How would you describe the look and feel of this short?*
>
> "The film has been created using cel animation and Flash. We have used two different looks where the parts depicting Toah's home have been kept clean, simple, shades of blue, and the other side of the story has been depicted using darker colors, more details, grunge and subtle animation not to distract the visuals. Blue and green were used for the clean parts, whereas blacks, grey and brown [were used] for the polluting arts of the film."

September 6. The first theatrical trailer for *Shri Hanuman Chalisa* is released:

> Animated mythological poetry is on its way as Delhi-based Charuvi Design Labs, founded and spearheaded by Animation Film Maker Charuvi Agrawal, has recently rolled out the first trailer of their debut animated short based on the verses of *Hanuman Chalisa*.
>
> Titled *Shri Hanuman Chalisa*, this 12 minute, 20 second 3D animated poetry is adapted from *The Hanuman Chalisa* written by Indian poet Tulsidas and promises to spread a divine visual poetic experience. The teaser of this short was first screened in 2011 at SIGGRAPH film festival and since then has been doing its rounds in the international film festivals. The film had its world premiere at Palm Springs International Short Fest and Film Market—California (USA), an Oscar qualifying festival.

Checking around, there have been multiple live-action productions of *Shri Hanuman Chalisa* over the years. Hanuman is the Hindu monkey god, or monkey-headed and –tailed human god. He is often shown fighting inhuman demons, as he is in the trailer for this film. The Indian poet Tulsidas lived from 1497 or 1532 to 1623. Most sources recognize the 1497 date as correct, although this would have made him 126 years old when he died. Hindus argue that this is perfectly likely since Tulsidas praised Hanuman throughout his life, and Hanuman probably extended his life span. This trailer does not exhibit ANY motion besides drifting dust, but the monsters are monstrous, and the 3D effect without glasses is surprisingly successful.

September 16. The Amul Girl is apparently one of India's best-known TV advertising mascots, similar to Tony the Tiger or the Trix Rabbit in America. Toonz Animation gives the Amul Girl mascot a 3D makeover in TV commercials:

> Trivandrum-based Toonz Animation has created the 3D avatar of the iconic, utterly, butterly delicious Amul Girl. Conceived in 1967, this young, chubby Indian girl dressed in a polka dotted frock with blue hair and a half pony has been the face of Indian dairy brand Amul since. And now, after more than 4 decades of fascinating us in her hand-drawn form, the Amul Girl has adorned a 3D avatar in Amul's latest TVC. Released by the Gujarat Cooperative Milk Marketing Federation, the TVC is created by Kailash Pictures, whereas the 3D animation, motion graphics and compositing have been delivered by Toonz Animation. The live action cum animation TVC is currently airing on leading television channels.

I have recently seen *Cloudy With a Chance of Meatballs 2*, and I can't watch this without thinking of a deep male voice saying, "Butter!"

September 25. *Krishna aur Kans* (*Krishna versus Kans*, Krishna's evil uncle), Reliance Animation's CGI theatrical feature that was released across India in several languages in August 2012, has come to Indian TV:

> & Pictures, the newly launched movie channel of Zee Entertainment, is all set to telecast India's finest animated feature film *Krishna aur Kans*. [...] The film is directed by Vikram Veturi and has a stellar voice cast who are among the finest actors of our time.

This deserves to be called "India's finest animated feature film", even if it is a Hindu religious film about the first ten years of Krishna's life that will be meaningless to most Americans. It was shown in America for one week in one theater in Norwalk, CA, under the title *Hey Krishna* to qualify for the Oscars.

September 26. *Mahavir—The Protector* (the Hindu gods as American-style costumed superheroes):

Kolkata-based Virtualinfocom is currently working on their first IP, a 2D animation movie, *Mahavir—The Protector*. This 90-minute movie will be targeted at a wider range of audience between the age group from 5 to 25 years old. The studio started working on several aspects of this movie in 2011. Currently in production, the feature is tentatively slated for mid 2014.

Kalki (incarnation of Lord Vishnu) and Gadura (Kalki's godfather) are the main characters of the movie. The other secondary characters are Shiva, Vishnu, Durga, Ganesh, Kartik, Yamraj, Gadura, Blood Seed (Rakta Beej), Nova, Taraka, Rakhshashi, Kumbhakarna, Indra, Maya, Kali, and Klesh.

The movie follows the story of the super power called Kalki, born in 2124 to destroy the evil spirits in and around the earth using his ultimate powers. As per the story line, before Kalki's birth, seven devotional Sadhus did a "Maha-Nirvana" Yagya. These sadhus had super powers they used to call their protector, but one of them chose not to do so and left the Yagna area, so the power was born but it had no body. The power is in the form of a spirit who can't take part in any mortal world, and who is seeking for a pure body.

After referring to several American superhero comic books, by the look of the character design, I can recognize the elephant-headed Ganesh, and I assume the sinister-looking black-clad warrior is Shiv. I would guess Kali, the goddess of death, but she's female. The third paragraph above, about the "Maha-Nirvana" Yagya, exceeds my knowledge of the Hindu religion.

Mahavir—The Protector may be a hit with Indian audiences, but I cannot begin to guess how it will play to Americans. Considering the box-office popularity of the current live-action Spider-Man, Iron Man, and Avengers movies, it could be very successful if the American editing and dub (no language is mentioned, but I assume that the film will be in Hindi) can take out the Hindu religious aspects, the way that the American 1961 version of *Alakazam the Great* changed Chinese mythological names to Hercules and Merlin the Magician. And assuming that the animation is up to American standards.

Chapter 6

加西生学由天谊 更

The Animated Olympics Mascots

The first Olympics to have a cartoon mascot as distinct from an emblem were the 1972 Summer Games in München, although the 1968 Winter and Summer Games both used a unique "proto-mascot" on their official stationery and press releases. The 1972 München mascot was Waldi, a multi-shaded blue dachshund in a gaudy sweater. However, Waldi didn't do much more than exist as a mascot and Waldi plush dolls.

The 1976 Winter Games in Innsbruck (Schneemann, an anthropomorphized snowball) and Summer Games in Montréal (Amik, a beaver) took the concept of mascots further in merchandising with dolls, cloth patches, pins, etc., but these were still little more than one image used over and over.

It was with the 1980 Summer Games in Moscow that the Olympic mascot was given a personality and really came alive. Probably everyone on Earth has seen Misha the bear cub. The Moscow Olympics Organizing Committee took special care to make him a genuine personality.

Misha was "born" in 1977 when the Moscow Olympics Organizing Committee held a contest to design the 1980 Summer Games mascot. The contest was first conducted by a popular TV program, *Animal World*, and a magazine, *Soviet Sport*, to choose the type of mascot. The majority of the 45,000 letters recommended the Russian national symbol, the brown bear. The Committee next asked 60 artists recommended by the Artists' Union of the U.S.S.R. to submit designs featuring a bear. The winning design was submitted by Victor Chizhikov, a popular illustrator of children's books. It was of a smiling bear cub wearing a belt of the five colors of the Olympic rings (blue, black, yellow, green, and red), with an Olympic-rings golden buckle. It reportedly took Chizhikov six months to draw a hundred variations of Misha for use in all poses. Chizhikov's flat drawings were developed into a three-dimensional model by another artist, Victor Ropov. Misha was given such an extensive backstory that the MOOC threw most of it out as superfluous, keeping only Misha's full name, Mikhail Potapych Toptygin, and his birthday, December 19, 1977 (which was actually the date that he was approved by the MOOC as the 1980 Summer Games' official mascot).

Misha was the first Olympics mascot to be merchandized in too many forms to list, and to be immortalized in many forms. There are still at least three Misha statues in Kiev, Ukraine. (Or Kyïv; now that it is independent, Ukraine is pushing to make everyone aware that Ukrainian rather than Russian spellings are preferred.) Misha has also retained his popularity longer than any other Olympics mascot. There have continued to be Misha plush dolls in Russia, and when Sochi was chosen as the site of the 2014 Winter Games, there was a huge demand throughout Russia to make Misha its mascot again. When a cartoon polar bear was chosen as one of three official mascots (White Misha the polar bear, Zaika the winter hare, and Leopard the snow leopard), he was officially declared to be Misha's grandson. (This did not save him from an accusation of plagiarism by Misha's creator, Victor Chizhikov. "It's exactly the same as mine: the eyes, the nose, the mouth, the smile. I don't like being robbed," he has said publicly.)

Actually, this may be illegal. According to the by-laws of International Olympic Committee's Rule 50 governing the use of mascots:

> 50.3. Any mascot created for the Olympic Games shall be considered to be an Olympic emblem, the design of which must be submitted by the OCOG to the IOC Executive Board for its approval. Such mascot may not be used for commercial purposes in the country of an NOC without the latter's prior written approval.

and:

> 50.4. The OCOG shall ensure the protection of the property of the emblem and the mascot of the Olympic Games for the benefit of the IOC, both nationally and internationally. However, the OCOG alone and, after the OCOG has been wound up, the NOC of the host country, may exploit such emblem and mascot, as well as other marks, designs, badges, posters, objects and documents connected with the Olympic Games during their preparation, during their holding and during a period terminating not later than the end of the calendar year during which such Olympic Games are held. Upon the expiry of this period, all rights in or relating to such emblem, mascot and other marks, designs, badges, posters, objects and documents shall thereafter belong entirely to the IOC. The OCOG and/or the NOC, as the case may be and to the extent necessary, shall act as trustees (in a fiduciary capacity) for the sole benefit of the IOC in this respect.

The mascot suits, animation production materials and prints, and any unsold merchandise are required to be destroyed, not sold. This is why the judges of the Russian nationwide design contest to select the 2014 Sochi Winter Olympics mascot, held September 1 to December 5, 2010, rejected a majority favorite among the 24,000 designs submitted: Ded Moroz, or Father Frost. The judges explained during the February 7, 2011, announcement of the winners that, according to the IOC Rules, all Summer and Winter Games mascots become the property of the IOC, and must be discontinued within the end of the calendar year after the completion of their games. Since Father Frost has been a traditional Russian folkloric character for centuries, nobody would want to give him up to the IOC and have him discontinued after the year's end. Therefore, Misha should have been withdrawn after the end of 1980.

Misha was the first mascot to be massively merchandised, on hundreds of items from children's baby bibs and toys to adults' household utensils and cigarette lighters. But what we are interested in is the animation. Misha has also been animated more than any other mascot.

The leading example was just before the 1980 games, in Баба-Яга против! (*Baba Yaga Protiv!*; *Baba Yaga Protests!*), a three-part, 9-minute-each theatrical cartoon directed by Vladimir Pekar at Soyuzmultfilm, and released during early 1980. Baba Yaga, the traditional Russian witch who lives in a forest in a walking hut on giant chicken legs, is jealous that Misha has been selected to be the Olympics mascot instead of her. She tries to kidnap him so she can replace him before he can light the Olympic torch, but her clumsy assistants, Gorynych the three-headed snake/dragon and Koschei the Deathless (two more folkloric villains), keep fouling up. *Baba Yaga Protests!* was shown throughout the Soviet Union and possibly Eastern Europe.

There were at least two other short animated appearances of Misha in the Soviet Union, both produced by Soyuzmultfilm. One was a 9¼-minute cartoon titled Кто получит приз? (*Who Will Get the Prize?*), in which the forest animals hold an Olympics-style foot race. Misha is clearly the fastest, but he keeps stopping to help out other animals such as a baby bird who has fallen out of its nest. An additional complication is a fox who cheats. Misha comes in last, but the other animals agree to declare him the winner because his unselfish helpfulness demonstrates the true Olympics spirit.

The other is a walk-on appearance at the conclusion (8'32" of 9'18") of *Nu, Pogodi!* #13, the popular series of the Wolf and the Hare that has been called the Russian equivalent of MGM's Tom and Jerry. The title is the Wolf's habitual signoff, which is usually translated as, "Just you wait!" or "I'll get you next time!" In #13, directed by Vyacheslav Kotyonochkin and released on May 17, 1980 (two months before the Games), the Wolf chases the Hare into the 1980 Olympics, and after the usual cartoon mishaps, both the Wolf and the Hare end up on the winners' stand where Misha presents them each with an award.

But the animated Misha seen around the world was Japanese, a 26-episode TV series titled *Koguma no Misha* (*Misha the Bear Cub*), directed by Yoshimichi Nitta at Nippon Animation. It was broadcast on TV Asahi on Saturdays from 7:00 to 7:30 p.m., from October 6, 1979, to March 29, 1980. Aside from using the Summer Olympics' mascot design that Nippon Animation had licensed, the TV serial was developed with all Japanese writers and cinematographers—the character designer was Isamu Kumada—and bore no connection with the Olympic Games in Moscow that summer.

The series is about young Misha and his parents, the Potapychs, who have just moved from a big city to the remote town (population: 99) of Himadabeya. Mr. Potapych is a former newspaperman who wants solitude to write a novel. Misha tries to adjust to a rural life and make new friends, but naturally there are problems with bullies and clannish adults who don't like strangers. Misha gradually wins acceptance among the proud loners. One continuing situation is that among Misha's first playmates are Nyago and Mirumiru, the son and daughter of Mr. Nekosuki the tapir inventor. Nyago becomes one of Misha's best friends, but Mirumiru develops a crush on him and becomes insanely jealous of the bear girl Natasha. Misha has to figure out how to let Mirumiru down gently. The whole cast are funny animals: adult and juvenile tapirs, foxes, tigers, storks, cats, hippopotamuses, and others. The conductor and engineer of the little train that brings the Potapychs to Himadabeya are gorillas. The program was best-known for giving Misha a young girl friend, the polar bear Mayor's daughter Natasha. Several reviewers commented that this was more than he'd been given in the Soviet Union.

Aside from being broadcast in Japan, *Koguma no Misha* was shown in France, Italy, Mexico, Portugal, and Spain. It was dubbed into Arabic and Farsi, and was reportedly popular throughout the Arabic-speaking world. 1980 advanced to 1984, and the Summer Olympic Games were held in Los Angeles. Both the United States Olympic Committee and the Los Angeles Olympic Organizing Committee agreed that there was only one man, or company, to design the 1984 mascot: Walt Disney Productions. It should be noted that Card Walker, the Disney Company's chairman of the board, was also on the LAOOC executive committee. Disney assigned its Art Director, C. Robert (Bob) Moore, to design the mascot; his last important job before he retired. While Moore was not quite ordered to make an American bald eagle the mascot, the vast majority of the organizers felt that the mascot should officially represent all America, not just Los Angeles or California. Disney historian Jim Korkis quotes Moore as later saying:

> We even thought of oranges and palm trees. We tried animated cactuses, snakes and turtles, but they were all symbolic of being slow, something the Olympics wanted to avoid. We considered a buffalo but decided on the eagle.

The buffalo (American bison) was the only other choice seriously considered, but Moore felt that when a buffalo was anthropomorphized to stand on two legs, it looked top-heavy. The eagle had its own problems; it looked too stern or martial, and it lacked hands. Moore was asked to design a child-friendly "cuddly, patriotic eagle", and he successfully designed the wings so they could double as arms and hands. Sam the Olympic Eagle was unveiled to the public on August 4, 1980.

Sam's popularity from 1980 until summer 1984 should not need repeating. If he was not merchandised more heavily than Misha, it is only because both were so heavily merchandized that the difference is inconsequential. A major problem that Sam never overcame was that his head of white feathers made him look like a senior citizen. He may have been cuddly, but he came across at best as a kindly old man. Whether Moore ever tried to design Sam as a child or an athletic youth is not known, but despite being shown as participating in all of the Summer Olympics sports, he was unmistakably an older adult. Although he was designed by a Disney artist, there was never any serious demand in America to animate him. Sam was withdrawn according to IOC rules at the end of the year after the 1984 Summer Games were over, and was soon forgotten.

Animator Michael Sporn commented:

> In 1984 I was contacted by two executives from Warner Bros. who hired me to develop a low budget script for an animated feature that starred Sam the Eagle. I had a ball making a parody of [Alfred Hitchcock's] North by Northwest with the Eagle caught in a cross country race where enemy agents were out to stop the future mascot of the Olympics. The climax took place in Disneyland ("No problem," they promised me.) Since there was only 11 months to actually make the film in time for the Olympics, they got nervous and pulled out at the last minute. I ended up making Dr. DeSoto instead and got an Oscar nomination.

I would imagine that an additional problem would have been the IOC's requirement that all prints of the film would have had to be destroyed or turned over to the IOC by the end of the year after the 1984 Olympics.

But Sam did become a star of a weekly TV cartoon series, once more in Japan: Eagle Sam, which ran weekly for 51 episodes directed by Hideo Nishimaki and Kenji Kodama, at Dax International. The series was broadcast on Tokyo Broadcast System (TBS) on Thursdays from 7:00 to 7:30 p.m., from April 7, 1983, to March 29, 1984.

Unlike *Koguma no Misha*, *Eagle Sam* never played outside Japan. Those who have seen it have wondered how it ever came to play IN Japan! The obvious answer, whether true or not, was that someone must have decided to get revenge against America for World War II.

Eagle Sam was a gun-waving private investigator. (Everyone knows that all Americans are gun-happy.) He had a human secretary, Canary Karina, who may or may not have been supposed to be pretty—with character designer Yoshio Kabashima's art style, it was hard to tell—but there was no doubt about the amount of cleavage she showed. Canary appeared in at least one nude shower scene, and in the closing credits (shown every week), Sam deliberately ripped off her mini-skirt to expose her white panties. Sam and Canary were always accompanied on their cases by Gosling, her slingshot-wielding kid brother. Sam was portrayed as the only one in Olympic City (a thinly-disguised stereotype of Hollywood) who could solve any crime or catch any criminal, because the police were too busy eating doughnuts, playing golf, or beating up innocent people. The police uniform's badge was a Star of David. Naturally, Chief Albatross and Officer Bogie (or Bogey) didn't like to be shown up, so they—with Albatross's daughter Chichi—were always trying to sabotage Sam. Usually, Albatross thought up the schemes and assigned Bogie to carry them out, but Bogie seldom got further than being distracted by Canary's cleavage. When Sam got into a tight spot, he would toss his Olympic Hat with the five glowing rings into the air, reach into it, and pull out whatever he needed. The villain who gave Sam the most trouble was the disrespectful, jive-talkin', skateboarding, shades-wearing cockroach, Gokuro, who drove him crazy with his sassy but legal mockery. (Cockroach in Japanese is gokiburi.) Other characters were Mr. Pelican the hippie and Thunderbird the weight-lifter.

A lot of anime fans do not believe this series existed, but the opening and closing credits are on YouTube to prove it. *Eagle Sam* was for little children, and despite its unbelievable scenario, it was shallow and boring. The 1988 Summer Games were in Seoul, and the 1988 mascots designed by Kim Hyun were a male and female pair of cartoon adolescent Amur tigers, Hodori and Hosuni (although Hosuni was usually ignored), looking very friendly and animate-able. Hodori appeared in a TV cartoon series on South Korea's MBC network titled 달려라 호돌이 (*Ride Hodori*) that was apparently never seen outside the country. Hodori also appeared in animated TV advertisements for commercial products. This brings us to 1992 and the Summer Games in Barcelona. A major shift in the public attitude toward Olympic mascots had occurred by then. The public was complaining about the overcommercialization of the Olympic games through cute mascots designed to sell merchandise. As a result, Javier Mariscal, the designer of the 1992 Summer Games mascot (chosen by the COOB in a contest from six finalists during 1987), took care to make him, if not ugly, at least not cute. The 1992 mascot was Cobi, a "modernist", stylized-to-the-point-of-abstract-art Pyrenees Sheepdog puppy drawn in the style of artist Pablo Picasso's cubism, and unveiled to the public on January 29, 1988. His name was a play on that of the Barcelona Olympics Organizing Committee (COOB in Spanish). "The name was chosen because it is simple and easy to pronounce in most languages." Cobi was derided as ugly at first, but the people of not just Catalonia but all Spain came to love him. And despite being designed to be non-commercial, there was a ton of merchandising "Cobiana" Cobi souvenirs; so many that Cobi reportedly became "the most profitable mascot in the history of the Olympics." (But an article in the Business section of Britain's *The Independent*, May 2, 2013, says that the 1992 Barcelona merchandising "only" brought in $17,200,000, and calls 1992 "arguably the last games of the non-commercial era. ... From 1996, no games would make less than two and a half times that amount.")

The merchandising included a TV cartoon program, *The Cobi Troupe* (in English, but also known by the Catalan translation *Cobi e Sua Turma*). The director was Olivia Borricon, and the producer was Spain's big animation studio, BRB Internacional S.A. in Alcobendas, near Madrid. There were 26 episodes, aimed for young children, broadcast during 1992. Cobi starred with his girlfriend, Petra, who was even more stylized—she had no arms, to represent the Paralympics. Other members of Cobi's gang were Jordi, Olivia, Cachas, Rosi, and Bicho, all carefree youths, and their adversary was Doctor Normal, a gloomy adult. "The rights were bought by 24 television channels." There were also six issues of a 48-page *The Cobi Troupe* comic book published during 1991-92.

By 1996, the anti-merchandisers were out in full force, and they saw to it that the 1996 Summer Games in Atlanta had a mascot that could not possibly be merchandised: the abstract, bright blue Izzy, formally Whatizit, so-named for "What is it?", and designed by John Ryan of DESIGNefx. Hah! The 1996 Summer Games' merchandising brought in $91,000,000, with Izzy stuff responsible for no small part of that—despite his being possibly the most reviled Olympics mascot of all time. Some criticisms were "the blue maggot" and "the sperm in sneakers". Matt Groening quipped that Izzy looked like "the bad marriage of the Pillsbury doughboy and the ugliest California Raisin." Wikipedia says:

A popular joke that circulated in Atlanta around the end of the 1996 games stated that the blue line painted on Peachtree Road (which actually designated the route for the Olympic Marathon) was "Izzy's ass being dragged out of town."

Reportedly, the Atlanta Centennial Olympic Properties (ACOP) officials were swayed by the arguments of computer animators that, with the latest technology of 1996, they could create the most impressive CGI animations and morphing with an abstract, brightly-colored blob. Apparently, there were brief TV commercials in CGI, although I have not been able to find out any information about them.

Izzy was designed for traditional cartoon animation by Guy Vasilovitch of the Film Roman studio in Hollywood. He only achieved one bit of memorable animation. The ACOP commissioned a half-hour TV special titled *Izzy's Quest for Olympic Gold*, produced by Carol Corwin (no director credit is given) at Film Roman, shown on TNT (naturally; Atlanta is Ted Turner's home base) on August 12, 1995. I wrote an extensive article about it for *Animation World Magazine* in July 1996, with this plot synopsis from Frankie Kowalski:

> The special, *Izzy's Quest For Olympic Gold*, that aired on Atlanta-based Turner Network Television (TNT) on August 12, 1995, was a two-part show, and has also been distributed internationally. It begins with Izzy, a mischievous teenager who lives in a whimsical world inside the Olympic Torch. In this land, the people—called Whatizits—are charged with the responsibility of keeping the spirit of the Olympic Games, and the Torch, shining bright. Never one to just go with the flow (that's why I like him), Izzy causes an uproar when he wants to leave the Torch to be a part of the Olympic Games he had heard so much about. Izzy must prove himself worthy and learn important lessons about the purpose and history of the games by earning the five Olympic Rings—Perseverance, Integrity, Sportsmanship, Excellence, and Brotherhood. (This meaning comes from a story session at Film Roman. In fact, the rings stand for the colors of the five continents participating in the Olympics.)

Despite the report of *Izzy's Quest For Olympic Gold* being distributed internationally, no source says where.

There was also a video game, *Izzy's Quest for the Olympic Rings*. The TV special is not on YouTube, but 2 minutes and 25 seconds of footage from the video game is. (If anyone knows where to find a copy of *Izzy's Quest for Olympic Gold*, please let me know.)

Blogger Jason LeGault has said:

> After the 1996 Olympics...[t]here were many attempts to keep Izzy popular, including updating his look and promoting him with his

own roller coaster at Busch Gardens Williamsburg. (The name Izzy is no longer displayed on the ride.) But like most of the other Olympic mascots, once they're used they're not used again.

By 2000, the anti-merchandising forces seemed to have given up. The 2000 Summer Games in Sydney had three cute cartoon mascots, apparently designed by Matt Hatton and Jozef Szekeres for their merchandisability: Syd the duckbilled platypus, named for Sydney and representing water power and "the energy and vigour of Australia (and Australians)"; Ollie the kookaburra, named for the Olympics and representing the air power and the spirit of friendliness and generosity; and Millie the echidna, named for the new millennium and Australia's technological advancement and representing earth power.

Hah! again. The anti-merchandising forces only appeared to have given up. They reappeared with a particularly Aussie slant. Millie, with her distinctive echidna's snout, was popularly renamed "Dickhead". But the worst insult of all was that the three official mascots were upstaged by a parody. Sydney cartoonist Paul Newell created Fatso, the Fat-Arsed Wombat as a protest against the overcommercialization of the Olympics. Fatso was publicized on the popular sports/comedy TV program, *The Dream with Roy and HG*, with a life-sized plush doll with an oversized rump on Roy and HG's desk. And Fatso was preferred over the official mascots by some of the Olympics athletes! When the Australian Olympic Committee tried to forbid any athletes from bringing unofficial mascots into the stadium, Fatso's popularity was assured. The AOC wisely backed down. Subsequently, there was a statue of Fatso at the Sydney Stadium (until it was stolen in 2010), and Fatso has appeared on an Australian postage stamp—just as a plushie being held by a member of the 2000 swimming team, but that was more than any of the three official mascots ever got.

Despite all this, neither Syd, Ollie, Millie, or Fatso were ever animated. The 2000 Olympics were the first Summer Olympics since 1980 to do without any animation.

The 2004 Summer Games in Athens had many people's (including mine) choice as the ugliest mascots of all time, Izzy notwithstanding. Phevos and Athena, brother (in blue tunic) and sister (in orange tunic), designed by Spiros Gogos of Paragraph Design, were based on a crude 7th century B.C. terracotta "daidala" doll used as both a children's toy and as a fertility symbol. NBC's Olympic host Bob Costas described them as looking like "a genetic experiment gone horribly, ghastly wrong." The Athens Organizing Committee was apparently really only interested in promoting the 2004 Summer Games as the followup to the original

Olympics in the 6th-century B.C., and not interested in modern merchandising; those Summer Games lost a lot of money. They were animated only in 30-second Greek TV promotions.

Animation returned with a vengeance to the 2008 Summer Olympics in Beijing. The BOCOG (Beijing Organizing Committee for the Games of the XXIX Olympiad) had the National Society of Chinese Classic Literature Studies select a mascot. The NSCCLS entrusted the task to Han Meilin, a prominent Chinese artist. He designed *five* ultra-cute anthropomorphized mascots, collectively known as the Fuwa good-luck dolls: Beibei the fish, representing water, prosperity, and the continent Europe (blue, female); Jingjing the panda, representing forests, happiness, and Africa (black, male); Huanhuan the fire spirit, representing the Olympic spirit and America (red, male); Yingying the Tibetan antelope, representing earth, good health, and Asia (yellow, male); and Nini the swallow, representing the sky/metal, good luck, and Oceania (green, female). Among the many international presentations, a Beijing Olympic Float featuring the five Fuwa at the 2008 Pasadena, California Rose Parade won the Theme Trophy for excellence in presentation of the Parade's theme, which was "Passport to the World's Celebrations".

Beijing's mascot animation seemed to be more for informational and promotional purposes than for merchandising. 福娃奥运漫游记/ *Fúwá Àoyùn Mànyóujì* (*The Olympic Adventures of Fuwa*) was an animated program of 100 eleven-minute episodes. The series was produced by the China Beijing TV Station/BTV and Kaku TV (a cartoon channel). It was shown on BTV in Beijing, on 100 other TV stations throughout China, on China's nationwide railroad videos, and on Beijing's public transportation system. Prior to being broadcast, Kaku TV presented copies to foreign embassies and major cities. Kaku TV later released a multilingual DVD in Chinese (Mandarin and Cantonese), English, French, Japanese, and Korean. *The Olympic Adventures of Fuwa* beat nearly 120 other competitors from 28 countries to win the Best Production award at the 2007 Asian Animation Comics Contest in Guiyang, China, on September 7-10, 2007. No production information is given other than that "creators from mainland China and Hong Kong collaborated to produce the series". The 100 episodes aired from August 8, 2007, to the "opening of the games", which was on August 8, 2008.

The cartoon's story began on the first episode's broadcast date, August 8, 2007. It featured an 8-year Beijing boy, Da You, getting the five Fuwa dolls as a birthday gift from his parents. The dolls come to life, and they and Da You have adventures that are learning experiences in Chinese history and culture, the history of the Olympic Games, and the preparations in Beijing from August 2007 to the Olympic Games in August 2008. There were also short (3-minute) animated introductions of the five Fuwas to promote the games.

The Olympic Adventures of Fuwa was seen throughout China, but the 2008 Summer Olympics animation seen most often in the West was probably a 2-minute TV cartoon shown by BBC Sport. At this time musician Damon Albarn and graphic artist Jamie Hewlett (of *Tank Girl* fame) were developing a stage adaptation of the 16th-century Chinese novel *Journey to the West*, titled *Monkey: Journey to the West*. The BBC commissioned Hewlett and Albarn to create a 2-minute cartoon, titleless but officially named *Journey to the East*, showing the traditional Chinese folk tale cast of Monkey, Pigsy, and Sandy hurrying to Beijing for the 2012 Summer Games. The short film was shown frequently on BBC Sport to advertise the BBC's coming coverage of the 2012 Summer Olympics, and as the title sequence for its coverage of the games from August 8 to 24. Since then, it has been shown often on YouTube and other internet sites.

The 2012 Summer Games in London returned to "impossible to commercialize" mascots, not that anyone expected the London Organising Committee of the Olympic Games (LOCOG) to not merchandise them. The two futuristic mascots were named Wenlock and Mandeville, after two English towns that held Olympic-type sporting events before the modern Olympics and Paralympics were established. They were the first Olympic mascots to have their own website.

The LOCOG turned the designing of its mascots over to Iris Worldwide, a London creative agency, which created a team led by Grant Hunter to do the job. Hunter designed two "dynamic, forward-looking" mascots to represent the Olympics and the Paralympics. The characters were then given to popular children's book author Michael Morpurgo, who was Children's Laureate from 2003 to 2005, to write a story around them. Morpurgo wrote *Adventures on a Rainbow* especially as an outline for a series of animated short films, establishing them as drops of steel from the final support girder for the new Olympic Stadium.

Hunter and Morpurgo both claimed that Wenlock and Mandeville were extremely popular with young children. The LOCOG's chairman, Lord Coe, also said, "We've created our mascots for children. They will connect young people with sport and tell the story of our proud Olympic and Paralympic history." They were not popular with adults, though. Critics immediately described them as looking like the offspring of a "drunken one-night stand between a Teletubby and a Dalek", and "Izzy's revenge". Comparisons were made with Kang and Kodos, the two green aliens out to conquer Earth in the "Treehouse of Horror" episodes of the satirical TV program *The Simpsons*. Fun was made of each mascot's gigantic single eye, meant to symbolize modern man's all-seeing cameras on cel phones everywhere, and the taxi lights on their foreheads. "Both Wenlock and Mandeville share yellow lights on their foreheads, which act as homages to the famous yellow London taxis."

There have been dozens of photo-edited parodies. *The New York Times* said in a story on March 27, 2012:

> Wenlock and Mandeville, which purportedly represent drops of steel from a girder of Olympic Stadium, entered the modern-day wilds of photo-editing software and a flourishing culture of online snark. They have been turned into Queen Victoria. They emerge from the eyes of Gordon Brown, the former prime minister of Britain. They are drooping objects in a Salvador Dalí painting. Sometimes they're plaid, sometimes they're striped. Often, they are not appropriate for a family newspaper.

The sports blog *Deadspin* invited readers to submit parodies of Wenlock and Mandeville. Among the entries: a mascot as Gene Kelly from *Singin' in the Rain*, the two mascots strolling across the street alongside the Beatles in their album cover for *Abbey Road* and the mascots helping soldiers raise the American flag at Iwo Jima.

More importantly, the public ignored Wenlock and Mandeville merchandise. *Mail Online* reported:

> Based upon blobs of steel and featuring a single eye each, less-than-cuddly mascots Wenlock and Mandeville were designed to symbolise the 2012 Games with their Olympic Ring-inspired friendship bracelets, and featured a nod to the capital in the form of London "taxi lights" on their heads. But the public failed to warm to the strange figures and a whole host of unsold Wenlock and Mandeville branded souvenirs and collectibles are now gathering dust on toyshop shelves. Hornby has knocked £96 off the price of a 12-pack of London 2012 die-cast Wenlock or Mandeville figurines, which are now on sale for £23.88, while many single figurines—originally priced £9.99—are now selling for £2.99.

But Wenlock & Mandeville's animation was designed for children. It was directed by Mario Cavalli and produced at the London offices of Crystal CG International, a multi-national CGI provider headquartered in Beijing, which had produced the CGI films shown at the 2008 Summer Olympics. Crystal CG International developed Michael Morpurgo's story into four short films designed to be shown on the LOCOG's website, on Vimeo and YouTube, and in Odeon cinemas throughout Britain (373 screens) at Odeon Kids Club screenings during the month of release. The four films were:

- *Out of a Rainbow* (May 2010; 4:17)
- *Adventures on a Rainbow* (March 2011; 4:54)
- *Rainbow Rescue* (November 2011; 5:00)
- *Rainbow to the Games* (May 2012; 16:47)

Crystal CG International said in a press release just after the release of the first film:

> Mario Cavalli recently completed direction of the Michael Morpurgo scripted OUT OF A RAINBOW, launching the London 2012 mascots, Wenlock and Mandeville. The mascots were developed and designed by Iris London over the preceding 18 months, with animation on the 3 min 45 sec film completed within a breakneck 10 week schedule, from design and storyboard to completion and launch on May 19th. Cavalli designed the non-mascot characters, working with Teddy Hall on maquettes and Pete Western on storyboard. Production design and backgrounds by Neil Ross, animation by Crystal CG. Editing by Richard Graham. Original score and orchestration by Tommy Hewitt Jones. Voice over read by Simon Russell Beale. The film was produced by Barnaby Spurrier. Within 48 hours of launch, the movie on the official LOCOG mascots' site had already clocked up 750,000 unique hits, while the same video on YouTube was the "most watched" in the last 24 hours.

The running story, developed largely through pantomime against a full orchestral background score, was that the old steelworker George retires after finishing construction of the final support girder for the new Olympic Stadium. He takes two spilled drops of steel as souvenirs. He bicycles home to his wife and twin ten-year-old grandchildren. During the night, he gets the idea of turning the steel drops into futuristic action figures for the children. The futuristic figures magically come to life and soar off on rainbows to begin setting up the 2012 games. In the subsequent films, the twins help Wenlock and Mandeville round up the athletes (CGI depictions of the known contestants), keeping in touch with the mascots on their rainbows via their cel phones. When a terrible storm destroys the twins' school library, Wenlock and Mandeville call on the athletes (more CGI depictions of the British Olympics Team members) to help restore it. Wenlock and Mandeville are accidentally locked in a huge cargo container being shipped to Rio de Janeiro, on the eve of the games. The twins, with the help of a young adult bicyclist friend, rescue them in time to get to the games.

That brings us up to date. The 2016 Summer Games will be held in (where else?) Rio de Janeiro. The Rio 2016 Organising Committee for the Olympic and Paralympic Games has announced that there will be two mascots, and they will be unveiled during the second half of 2014. Stay tuned to see if they will be animated.

Chapter 7

加西生学由天谊 光

Cartoons, Real and Suggested

Animals That Should Be Animated

The earliest animated cartoon that I can remember seeing was Disney's *Pinocchio*, on its first rerelease in October 1945, just before my fifth birthday. My mother, who was 101 years old last September, says that I'm wrong; she took me as a babe in arms to see *Bambi* with her. I will take her word for it. *Bambi* was released in August 1942; I was just over 1½ years old. I really do not remember it at all.

Even though *Pinocchio* was the earliest animated theatrical feature that I can remember, there were plenty of other funny animals from my fifth birthday until I entered my adolescence, theatrically and in the comics. Theatrically, there were all the cartoon shorts with the Disney stars; MGM's *Tom & Jerry* and *Droopy Dog*; the Warner Bros. funny animals; Terrytoons' *Mighty Mouse* and *Heckle & Jeckle* and *Gandy Goose & Sourpuss* and *Little Roquefort & Percy*; Famous' *Herman & Katnip*; and Lantz's *Woody Woodpecker* and *Chilly Willy*. I was vaguely aware that other funny animals that I was familiar with in the comic books, such as *Baby Huey* and the *Fox & the Crow*, were supposedly based on popular theatrical cartoon characters, but I do not remember ever seeing them on the big screen.

The newspaper comic strips and comic books offered lots more. I dimly remember *Mickey Mouse* and *Donald Duck* fighting Nazi spies and involved with Home Front themes, but most of my memories are of post-war stories. Other comic book funny animals such as *Super Rabbit* fought the Nazis, too. I read plenty of superhero comics during my preadolescence—*Captain Marvel, Superman* (I remember what a thrill it was when *Superboy* #1 appeared) and *Batman*, the Justice Society of America in *All-Star Comics*—but my favorites were the funny animal titles: *Walt Disney's Comics & Stories*, the *Mickey Mouse* and *Donald Duck* one-shots; Dell's *Animal Comics* where I first read the works of Walt Kelly, and other licensed characters who appeared in more adventurous plots than in their theatrical cartoons, or who weren't in theatrical cartoons at all (by that time), like *Andy Panda & Charlie Chicken* and *Oswald Rabbit*.

My favorites of the other funny animal comic books were most of the DC titles: *Animal Antics, Funny Stuff*, the later *Comic Cavalcade* issues, *Real Screen Comics* with the Fox & the Crow, and especially anything written & drawn by Sheldon Mayer. My earliest comic-book hero, who I wanted to grow up to be just like, when I was five or six years old, was Mayer's Amster the Hamster, a short con-man who could talk ANYbody (usually bigger characters) into ANYthing! As a five- or six-year-old surrounded by big adults, I thought that this would be a wonderful talent to possess. I later learned that Amster the Hamster was a funny-animal version of W. C. Fields. But all of Mayer's funny animals were hilariously funny with snappy dialogue: Doodles Duck and his bratty nephew Lemuel, Dizzy Dog, Buttons Bunny, Gus Goose, McSnertle the Turtle, Bo Bunny & Skinny Fox (who were a funny-animal Abbot & Costello), the Three Mousketeers, even the one-shot characters like Ferenc the Fencing Ferret. (I did not know it at the time, but Mayer also wrote but did not draw many of DC's superhero stories.) .

Decades later, when I was writing a special funny-animal theme issue of *Amazing Heroes* (#129, November 1987), I was thrilled to get the chance to personally interview Sheldon Mayer about his funny animals. I asked which of them had been his favorite:

> None of 'em! I thought the whole idea of funny animals is stupid! They would've been better as funny humans like Henry Aldrich or Jerry Lewis, or kids like the Our Gang bunch. Unless the plot required them to be tiny fantasy people, when you could make 'em human-looking elves or pixies. But DC wanted funny animals and assigned me to draw some, so I did."

Oh.

In addition to DC's comic books and Dell's (or Western Printing's) Disney titles, my favorite funny-animal comics were ACG's now-forgotten *Giggle Comics* and *Ha Ha Comics*. *Giggle* starred Superkatt, an ordinary housecat who impersonated a costumed hero in his owner's baby's bonnet and diaper. *Ha Ha* featured Robespierre, a black alley cat who was always getting into trouble with his yellow, brawny but impulsive pal Tiger. Aside from those series, with Superkatt signed by Dan Gordon and Robespierre by Ken Hultgren, *Giggle* and *Ha Ha* were filled with funny but interchangeable funny animal short stories by Gordon and Hultgren, and by Jack Bradbury and Don "Arr" Christiansen and Jim Tyer and others. I found out years later that they were all part of a workshop of moonlighting or ex-animation artists organized by Gordon to provide funny animal comics for publishers without their own in-house artists. Gordon had been with the Fleischer Studio (he has a writer credit on some of Fleischer's *Superman* cartoons), and quit when Paramount closed Fleischer's studio in Miami and moved the animators back to New York. Hultgren's regular job was with Disney; he was most famous for designing the Id monster that Disney's Joshua Meador animated for the April 1956 s-f movie *Forbidden Planet*.

Nobody seems to know how or why, but there was a single *Superkatt* animated cartoon, the May 1947 Columbia Phantasy Cartoon *Leave Us Chase It*. It was definitely based on the *Giggle* comic book series: a cat is inspired by reading the comic book stories to don a baby bonnet and diaper. A generic housecat-chases-mouse story follows, showing none of the imagination of Gordon's comic-book series. The cartoon's story is credited to Cal Howard, who was one of Dan Gordon's crew of moonlighting animation studio personnel. Maybe Howard pushed the cartoon to try to get an animated series for his pal Gordon's character. Who knows?

My family got its first television set just in time for the premiere of the first animated TV cartoon, *Crusader Rabbit*, on KNBH in Los Angeles on August 1, 1950. I was 9¾ years old, and I was mesmerized. I watched the five-minute episodes so religiously that I can still sing the advertisement jingle from the dog food commercials regularly shown during it:

Feed him Dr. Ross Dog Food; do him a favor.
It's got more beef, and it's got more flavor.
It's got more flavor 'cause it tastes the way it should;
Dr. Ross Dog Food is doggone good!
Fido knows best ... ARF!
Fido knows best ... ARF!

I wonder if the animated TV commercial was also made by Alex Anderson's and Jay Ward's Television Arts Productions?

I liked *Crusader Rabbit* (the original TAP 1949-51 black-and-white series; I was in college by the time the Cartoon Spots 1957-59 color series was broadcast) so much that when I began to get a reputation for writing articles about Japanese animation, I took some time out to research an article about *Crusader Rabbit*. ("2½ Carrots Tall, Television's First Animated Cartoon Star. Pt. 1, The Story Behind Crusader Rabbit", the history of the two series' production, in *Comics Scene* #6, November 1982; and "2½ Carrots Tall, Television's First Animated Cartoon Star. Pt. 2, The Stories of Crusader Rabbit", plot synopses of all the serials, in *Comics Scene* #7, January 1983.) It was a joy to talk face-to-face or in telephone interviews with most of the voice actors and production people who had made both series. (Jay Ward declined to be interviewed, though.) Everybody loved Alex Anderson and Jay Ward; everybody shut up or had nothing printable to say about Shull Bonsall, who produced the color series, and who had the foulest mouth of all and boasted about how he had screwed people. Jerry Fairbanks, the producer who took TAP's animation and sound tracks and produced them into films for TV broadcasting, was almost 80 years old and said, "That long ago...I just don't remember much. But I still have my scrapbooks, and you can look through them." A GOLD MINE! I sure hope that Fairbanks' scrapbooks went to some archive upon his death instead of being thrown out.

Fairbanks had the original memos, correspondence, and press clippings for everything: Anderson's and Ward's business trips from San Francisco to NBC in New York in 1948 to try to sell their proposed three-segment *The Comic Strips of Television* series; NBC's liking only the *Crusader Rabbit* segment (another segment that NBC turned down was *Dudley Do-Right*, which Ward used later in *Rocky and His Friends*), but being willing to buy it only if they had Jerry Fairbanks in Los Angeles produce it (NBC and Fairbanks had a sweetheart arrangement); Fairbanks' efforts all during 1949 to sell *Crusader Rabbit*, which consisted mostly of exaggerated press releases that implied the whole series of 130 five-minute episodes (65 episodes were added later) was ready for broadcast, while TAP was still churning out the cels and voice dubbings (one fascinating detail was that Fairbanks tried to make the limited animation sound like a cutting-edge new technological advance: "new Teletoon animation process delivers the quality of theatrical animation at a fraction of the cost" (I wonder if anyone in Canada's and France's TV industries knows of this prior use of "Teletoon"?; Bob Ganon, who worked on both the black-and-white and the color series, told me, "We just called it 'cheap animation'. Decide for yourself whether this is 'the quality of theatrical animation'."); Jay Ward's business trips from TAP in San Francisco to Fairbanks in L.A. to coordinate the production (Ward's full, legal name was J Troplong Ward); and so forth.

Well, I have wandered off-topic, which was supposed to be that while some of my favorite funny animals of my youth were in animated cartoons, many were not. It would have been great to see theatrical cartoons of Sheldon Mayer's characters, of Robespierre, of Superkatt as Dan Gordon had written him, of Fauntleroy Fox & Crawford Crow (yes, I know that they originated in Columbia's theatrical animated shorts, but I only encountered them in *Real Screen Comics*), of Dunbar Dodo & Fenimore Frog; of Nutsy Squirrel; and of Walt Kelly's Pogo Possum while the stories were still tremendously witty but still innocent children's comics, before they turned into adult social satire.

Is it too late? One of the greatest of the he-oughta-be-animated comic book characters of the 1950s was Disney's Scrooge McDuck, who was finally animated in Disney's TV cartoons in the late 1980s. Disney seems poised to do new things with 1927's *Oswald, the Lucky Rabbit* to keep him alive. The rights to Superkatt, et. al., are presumably available cheap...if it's not in the public domain by now.

Rats in Animation

Are rats "nicer" than mice?

In animation, it depends entirely upon the plot. Both mice and rats have to be anthropomorphized so much that any real difference does not matter.

In real life, rats are definitely smarter than mice. A "tame" mouse will not relate to humans at all; it just runs about aimlessly. A "tame" rat will react to humans, and exhibits much more curiosity.

I have admittedly very limited experience with both. I once visited a friend's friend who raised caged show mice for exhibition. My main memory is of a mother mouse who had just given birth to a litter of twelve. When she lay down to suckle them, it looked like she was being mobbed by tiny insatiable hooligans.

I have a bit more experience with rats. Around 1980, the Los Angeles Science Fantasy Society decided to bid for the 1984 World Science Fiction Convention. The Worldcon is hosted by a different city's fan group each year, and is voted on two years in advance, with bidders campaigning during the two years before that; so we had to start campaigning in 1980 for the voting in 1982 for the 1984 convention. We won, so the LASFS began organizing the 1984 Worldcon in late 1982. I was a member of the organizational committee, and so was a fan named Alan Frisbie. Both of us had been LASFS members for several years, but we did not know each other outside the club's weekly meetings.

We usually had our Worldcon planning sessions at the LASFS clubhouse, but on one occasion Frisbie and I had something more involved to plan between us, so he invited me to his home to discuss it. He lived alone, and his living room was filled with floor to ceiling bookcases. He directed me to sit in a comfortable chair right by one of the bookcases. We were talking for awhile when there was a tiny sneeze right in my left ear. I turned my head, and was eyeball to eyeball with a large rat! Frisbie said casually, "Oh, that's my pet rat. She likes to explore around my house. She's probably curious about your hair cream or your earwax. If you hold out your arm, she'll crawl up it to sniff your head." So I did, and the rat did.

I thought that was a one-time occasion, but Frisbie started bringing his rat, Reynolds, to our Worldcon planning sessions. He wanted to make her the official mascot of the 1984 Worldcon, L.A.con II. I doubt that many of us really approved of the idea, but we figured: it's late 1982, the convention is in Summer 1984, the average lifespan of a rat is two years and she's already several months old; sure, let's approve it to make Friz happy. She'll be dead by convention time. But she lived, and she died at L.A.con II, by a combination of extreme old age and nervousness at being petted by so many strange humans.

There was a smaller s-f convention, later during the 1980s, where one of the dealers was a "goth horror shop" festooned in black, selling skeletons of sparrows, skull earrings, and the like. It had a live "genuine plague rat" (a commercial laboratory rat) as a mascot. The rat was very popular with the children at the convention. That was where somebody pointed out that the rat was really interacting with the children, in comparison with hamsters or gerbils or guinea pigs or mice that never do anything except squeak to be fed or try to run away.

Friendly mice have long been popular in animation and children's books. Mickey Mouse. Gus and Jaq in Disney's *Cinderella*. Jerry of *Tom and Jerry*. Mighty Mouse. *The Mouse and His Child*. Miss Bianca, Bernard, and the Mouse Prisoners' Aid Society. *The Tale of Despereaux*. The anonymous mouse in *Mouse Hunt*. Speedy Gonzales. *An American Tail*. Nelvana's pre-*Rock & Rule* TV special, *The Devil and Daniel Mouse*. Amos Mouse in Disney's adaptation of Robert Lawson's *Ben and Me*. Ralph S. Mouse of *The Mouse and the Motorcycle*.

Rats? Just about the only positive rats have been in *The Secret of NIMH* movie adaptation of Robert C. O'Brien's novel *Mrs. Frisby and the Rats of NIMH*, and Pixar's *Ratatouille*. Okay, Templeton in *Charlotte's Web* and Roscuro in *The Tale of Desperaux*. There are Ratty in *The Wind in the Willows*, Rizzo the Rat of the *Muppets*, and Splinter in *Teenage Mutant Ninja Turtles*, but they are portrayed as unratlike as possible. Otherwise, there are the villainous Rattigan in *The Great Mouse Detective*, the villainous rats in Brian Jacques' *Redwall* series, the evil Botticelli Remorso in *The Tale of Desperaux*, the rats that attack the baby in *Lady and the Tramp*, and the rats in the horror movie *Willard* and its sequel *Ben* (although arguably they are only acting naturally; it's the human villain in *Willard* who makes them "evil", and Ben himself is heroic). When rats have been non-villains, they have usually been designed to look as unratlike and as human as possible, as in Nelvana's *Rock & Rule* and in Aardman Animations' *Flushed Away*. There have been semi-good guy rats as supporting characters, although they are usually portrayed more as amoral opportunists, such as Nick and Fetcher in *Chicken Run*.

There are several fantasies about rats that ought to make good animated movies. *Walter: The Story of a Rat* by Barbara Wersba is about a rat who lives in the home of a children's book writer, whose hero is a mouse. Walter undertakes a campaign to get her to write about rat heroes. In Terry Pratchett's *The Amazing Maurice and His Educated Rodents*, the cat Maurice talks a group of rats into joining him in a scam based on the Pied Piper legend; the rats will terrorize a town until a piper is paid to lead them away from it. But the rats and the human boy who is their stooge as the piper worry about the ethics of the plan. Suzanne Collins has written five novels in *The Underland Chronicles* about 11-year-old Gregor who falls into a land under New York City inhabited by talking animals based on NYC's vermin. The main animal characters are rats and bats. Tor Seidler has two children's books, *A Rat's Tale* and *The Revenge of Randal Reese-Rat*. In the first, when a NYC rat community is about to be destroyed by exterminators, the rats try to collect enough human money to buy them off. In the sequel, the rat heroes of the first are almost burnt to death in an arson fire. Haughty Randal Reese-Rat is suspected, and must become a detective to clear himself.

These and many other books would make excellent animated cartoon or CGI or stop-motion features, and would help break the stereotype that rats are always villains.

"Reynard the Fox" in Animation

One of the oldest talking-animal fables, as opposed to short parables such as Aesop's tale of the frogs that wanted a king (a.k.a. King Log and King Stork), is the Medieval folk tale of Reynard the Fox. Three of the earliest written versions known are *Ysengrimus*, a.k.a. *Reinardus Vulpes*, by the Flemish poet Nivardus in Latin around 1150, *Le Roman de Renart* by Pierre St. Cloud in Old French around 1170, and *Reinhard Fuchs* by Heinrich der Glïchezäre in Old German around 1180, but all are acknowledged to be based on then-well-known peasants' folk tales. William Caxton's English translation of 1481 is one of the earliest printed English books.

According to WikiFur:

> The stories are among the little political satire from the Middle Ages that still survives. The various animals were represented as various members of the aristocracy and the clergy. Human characters were often peasants.

The tale was doubtlessly so popular with commoners because it was a savage burlesque of the courts and politics of the nobility. It was also earthy; modern linguists study the manuscripts for their documentation of 12th-century insults, swearing, and scatology. At this time, Europe was divided among a series of kingdoms, duchies, counties, principalities, bishoprics, free cities, and others of shifting borders, with generally weak monarchs and strong nobles who were always jockeying among themselves for power. The portrayal of these proud and haughty dukes, lords, bishops, and cardinals as animals, constantly being tricked by Baron Reynard the fox, was amusing for centuries. There are carvings of the Reynard cast in Medieval churches and town halls. In France, 'reynard' replaced the older word for fox, 'goupil'.

The fox's name varies between Reynard, Renard, Renart, Reinard, Reinecke, Reinhardus, Reynardt, and Reynaerde. Other characters, the nobility at the court of King Leo the lion (in some versions King Nobel), include Isengrim the wolf, Bruin the bear, Chanticleer the rooster, Tybalt the cat (satirized by Shakespeare in *The Tragedy of Romeo and Juliet*), Baldwin the donkey, Grymbart the badger, Courtoys the hound, Cuwart the hare, Tyselyn the raven, Bellen the ram, Reynard's wife Hermeline, and many others. Some of these became "fixed" in their own right, such as Bruin for a bear and Chanticleer for a rooster.

The Reynard legend has been written many times over the centuries, and almost always illustrated. One of the earliest library books that I read, when I was six or seven years old, was Andre Norton's *Rogue Reynard; Being a tale of the Fortunes and Misfortunes and divers Misdeeds of that great Villain, Baron Reynard, the Fox, and how he was Served with King Lion's justice*, illustrated by Laura Bannon (Houghton Mifflin, June 1947).

It has been a natural for animation even before there was animation. One of the earliest efforts to show the Reynard tale in animated form was as a series of twelve Victorian lantern slides, which have become available on YouTube.

The length of the Reynard tale has made it more natural for features than for short films. In April 1937, *Le Roman de Renard* (a.k.a. *The Tale of the Fox*), a 67-minute stop-motion film by Ladislas and Irène Starevich, was finished in Germany. The animation had been completed in Paris in 1929 to 1930, but the Stareviches had considerable trouble getting the sound track made. This has been claimed as the world's third to sixth animated feature film, depending on how you consider earlier animated feature films. At any rate, it was released in Germany eight months before Disney's *Snow White and the Seven Dwarfs*.

The film is presented as "the oldest and most beautiful story known to us animals", as narrated by an elderly monkey dressed as a Medieval scholar. The scenario is credited to Irène Starevich, but it is essentially *Le Roman de Renart* as finalized in literary form by the Renaissance, especially in Wolfgang von Goethe's May 1794 *Reineke Fuchs* epic poem. By the 1920s, almost every standard edition of Goethe's poem had the 1840s illustrations by Wilhelm von Kaulbach, and the Starevich's stop-motion models look very similar to these.

The French release, with a French soundtrack, was in 1941; this is the most common version today. But any version is better-known in Europe than in America.

An anti-Semitic cartoon-animated "sequel", *About Reynaerde the Fox* (*Van den vos Reynaerde*), was made from 1941 to 1943 in the Nazi-occupied Netherlands. This was first published in a magazine in November 1937 by Robert van Genechten, a member of the Nationaal Socialistische Beweging (NSB), the Dutch equivalent of the German Nazi party. He intended it to be "New Literature for the New Order", full of Nazi doctrine. King Nobel has died, and the Animal Kingdom is under a regency led by Baldwin the Ass. A tribe of wandering rhinoceros merchants led by Jodocus enters the kingdom. The film makes blatant comparisons between the rhinos' nose-horns and the Nazi caricatures of big-nosed Jews, and the "Jod" of Jodocus is pronounced like the Dutch word for Jew. Jodocus flatters Baldwin, who is vain and foolish and easily tricked, and he appoints the rhinos to be the kingdom's tax collectors. The rhinos preach that a royal aristocracy is awfully old-fashioned; animals today are all for democracy and equality, where all are equal. All of the aristocratic animals intermarry, and their cat-chicken, bear-duck, and similar children are ugly and stupid, illustrating the Nazi doctrine of Racial Purity. Reynard, who has been quietly observing all this, realizes that the rhinos' goal is to weaken the animals' society so they can take it over. Reynard leads the aroused national socialist animal commoners to drive the rhinos into the sea and drown, and the kingdom is saved.

Ironically for van Genechten in 1937, the German literary censors rejected the novel, so it was only published in the Netherlands. The censors ruled that while van Genechten may have meant well, the International Jewish Menace and Racial Purity were too serious for parody, and that Reynard the fox was too well-established as a thief, trickster, and murderer to make a good Nazi role model. But when Germany conquered the Netherlands in 1940, the Nazis needed reliable Dutch collaborators to fill the occupation government. Van Genechten volunteered and became the new Procurator-General. In 1941, the Germans set up a new movie studio, Nederland Film, to make live and animated propaganda films. Van Genechten used his influence to see that the studio filmed his *About Reynaerde the Fox*, directed by Egbert van Putten, as well as to get his magazine story published as a novel (March 1941).

This was publicized as the Netherlands' first animated feature film, although it was a two-reeler only about 13 minutes long. Production was completed in April 1943, and a prestigious screening was held for NSB dignitaries and the film crew on April 25, 1943, at the Hague's UFA-theater, Asta. However, the film was never released. The German authorities, who controlled film distribution during the war, had the negative brought to Berlin, where it became lost during the fall of Berlin. But the film components were found in bits and pieces during the 1990s and 2000s, and the completed film was first shown at the Holland Animation Film Festival in Utrecht in November 2006 for an academic audience. The reviews were that it was very well-made, but very anti-Semitic. There were several changes from the novel, the major one being that the illustrations in the novel showed the cast as natural, unclothed, four-legged forest animals, while the animated cartoon has them as bipedal, medieval-clothes-wearing funny animals.

No reason was ever given for the non-distribution during World War II. My opinion is that the Dutch public's passive resistance to the German occupiers had increased so much by 1943 that the Germans felt that there would be a massive boycott of the heavy-handed propaganda cartoon, and that it would not be worth the critically-limited film stock to have prints made.

Walt Disney seriously considered for decades making a feature based on the Medieval folk tale, but with a difference. It was to be based not on *Le Roman de Reynard* but rather Edmond Rostand's February 1910 French play *Chantecler*, a satire on current French social pretension starring the vain rooster who believes that his crowing in the morning makes the sun come up. Reynard does not appear in the play at all.

Chantecleer went through two periods of serious consideration at Disney. The first was just after the success of *Snow White and the Seven Dwarfs*, from December 1937 to early 1938, when Disney was considering ideas for his second feature. He liked the idea of a barnyard comedy with a cast of pretentious roosters and chickens in fancy feathers, but nobody could develop a feature-length plot; and the foolishly arrogant Chanticleer was not a sympathetic character. Disney himself then suggested adding Reynard as a con-man fox to the plot to create more conflict, but the rooster still seemed too unsympathetic and the plot would not jell. Disney dusted off the project and gave it another try in 1941, 1945, and 1947, but with no further progress.

In 1961, after the success of *101 Dalmatians*, due largely to the work of Ken Anderson and Marc Davis (the designer and animator of Cruella deVil), Disney was looking for a new animation feature project. Davis became enthusiastic about reviving *Chanticleer* and turning it into a Broadway-style musical, as the studio did almost thirty years later with *The Little Mermaid*, using song-and-dance sequences to fill out the running time. Disney approved the idea, and for about six months *Chanticleer* was going to become an animated feature, with Reynard the fox as the manager of a dishonest traveling carnival. Then Disney confronted the fact that his theme park development in Florida was so expensive that he would have to cut his animation production expenses sharply. His studio had two features in full production, *The Jungle Book* and *Chanticleer*, but one would have to go. Disney chose to continue *The Jungle Book*. Reportedly, some of the *Chanticleer* animal character designs, especially of Reynard, were used in the 1973 Disney funny-animal feature *Robin Hood*.

Over twenty-five years later, Don Bluth, a defector from the Disney studio, made his own version of *Chanticleer*, the 77-minute *Rock*a*doodle*. It was even further removed from the *Reynard* legend, and did not feature any foxes. (As a commentator named "Tony" has pointed out, "Actually, there is a fox on *Rock*a*Doodle*. Chanticleer's Colonel Parker-type manager plays the Reynard role. It's easy to forget that he's a fox because he's drawn as fat, which foxes are usually not depicted as such.") But Charles Solomon has written a book about Disney's unfinished features, *The Disney That Never Was: The Stories and Art from Five Decades of Unproduced Animation* (Hyperion, December 1995), which contains many drawings from the studio's Animation Research Library of the never-finished *Chanticleer*.

In September 1986, *Moi Renart* (*I, Reynard*) debuted on French TV, running for 26 half-hour episodes directed by Jean Cubaud and animated at I.D.D.H. Angoulême (International Droits et Divers Holding) and Hanho Heung Up in Seoul. This modernization of the fable stars Renart as a young 20ish fox who comes from the countryside with his pet white monkey, Marmouset, to present-day Paris to live with his uncle Isengrim, an upper-class car salesman, and who falls in love with Hermeline, a vixen journalist. Renart is a bit of a rogue who creates a dummy business, l'Agence Renart, to carry out robberies, though he often steals from the seriously evil thieves. He becomes the adversary of Police Chief Chanticleer and Officer Tybalt. The art design by Pascale Moreaux is overly realistic; the characters look more like animal-headed humans rather than anthropomorphized animals. The series contains ingroup references to Japanese animated TV series imported into France by I.D.D.H., notably *Candy Candy*, although *Moi Renart* is aimed for adults as well as children (at least in the plots, not the poor animation).

In 1989, *Reineke Fuchs*, a 79-minute cartoon feature, appeared as a TV movie in West Germany. It was actually a West German-Chinese co-production, directed by Zhuang Minjin and He Yumen, and animated by the Shanghai Animation Film Studio. The German producer/co-director was Manfred Durniok. It was a straightforward adaptation of the 1794 poem by Wolfgang von Goethe, simplified for children ("Goethe für Kids"). Neither the animation quality nor the story adaptation did any honor to Goethe's poem.

In August 2005 a 90-minute CGI animated feature, *Le Roman de Renart*, directed by Thierry Schiel and produced by Oniria Pictures in Luxembourg, was released in Belgium, France, and Luxembourg, and later in other European countries. It was rich visually, but the story was strictly for children. This was one of those theatrical features in Europe that try to get an American release, as *Renart the Fox*, but become a direct-to-video kiddie DVD instead, retitled *The Adventures of Renny the Fox*. Watch with your mind turned off.

Zootopia and Other Animal Worlds

The third Disney D23 Expo for the studio's fans included an "Art and Imagination" presentation that showcased previews of Disney's planned theatrical features through 2016. At the far end was *Zootopia* (working title), a talking-animal picture about a fox, Nick Wilde, "framed for a crime he didn't commit", who is forced to team up with a Javert-like police-rabbit, Lt. Judy Hops (or Hopps), when they are both targeted by powerful criminals.

All of the animation news sites have reported on this planned release, and have shown the same publicity image of a noticeably bigger fox amidst a crowd of rabbits at an animal train terminal. Some have cropped the image to show only the fox and the rabbits, but others present the full view of the picture, which turns out to be important because it shows other, shadowy animals in the far background, such as an elephant, and indicates that they are huge compared to the fox and the rabbits!

The news sites note that this is the first Disney all-funny-animal feature since *Robin Hood* in November 1973. (Everyone seems to have forgotten about *Chicken Little* from November 2005. Wishful thinking?) Other theatrical features centered around talking animals have shown them as usually miniature imitation humans unnoticed in the human world, such as *The Great Mouse Detective* (July 1986) or *The Rescuers Down Under* (November 1990). But the Disney announcement claims that *Zootopia* will be original. "The twist is that the entire film is set in a world in which humans never existed (a la Pixar's *Cars*) and animals have built everything." *Entertainment Weekly* says that scheduled director

Byron Howard told the D23 audience:

> Just like New York has Chinatown and Little Italy, *Zootopia* has distinct regional neighborhoods like Tundratown, Sahara Square, Little Rodenta (the bad part of town, populated by vermin), and Burrowborough, populated by millions of bunnies.

This has set off speculation as to just what *Zootopia*'s original animal world will be like. The worlds of *Robin Hood*, *Chicken Little*, and such Disney TV animated programs as *DuckTales* and *TaleSpin* do not have any humans, but they all portray the funny-animal characters as surrogate humans: They are all roughly the same size, eat the same human diet, live in the same human civilizations, and so on. The *Zootopia* world will present the animals as all wearing clothes and walking upright, but what then? Will they stay true to their natural sizes? How do you design a single civilization for all animals from mice to elephants and giraffes? Will *Zootopia* acknowledge the difference between predator and prey animals?

The first animated features to star talking animals, rather than to use them as incidental characters like Jiminy Cricket in *Pinocchio* (February 1940), were the October 1941 *Dumbo* (circus animals) and the December 1941 *Mr. Bug Goes to Town* (garden insects). These were of the imitation-humans-in-the-human-world variety. The first to show a talking-animal world without humans was *Fritz the Cat* (April 1972). Again, this featured the animal cast as surrogate humans; they all lived in a human-style city, were the same size, and did nothing (including the birds) that humans would not be able to do. So for *Zootopia* to present something "different", it will have to SHOW something different: a realistic range of animal sizes, or a standoff between carnivores and herbivores with the omnivores mediating between the two, perhaps.

How original is this? In cinema, very. I don't believe that there are any animated or live-action features that have ever shown a true multi-animal civilization. In other media, it is fairly common. Online talking-animal comic strips like Bill Holbrook's *Kevin & Kell* (started September 1995), Jenner's *Doc Rat* (started June 2006), and John "The Gneech" Robey's discontinued *The Suburban Jungle* "starring Tiffany Tiger" (February 1999-November 2009), all feature(d) an animal civilization with "predation" by carnivores, under set laws. In comic books, Disney's *Li'l Bad Wolf* stories in *Walt Disney's Comics & Stories* featured Li'l Wolf and his Big Bad Wolf father, who was always trying to catch and eat Li'l Wolf's friends, the Three Little Pigs. In Belgian cartoonist Raymond Macherot's *Inspector Chaminou* series (one hardcover comic strip adventure, *Chaminou et le Khrompire*, 1965; sequels produced by others after Macherot's retirement in the 1990s under his supervision until his death), eating one's fellow-citizen is illegal in the Kingdom of Zoolande, but there is a criminal secret society of carnivores who kidnap and feast on the herbivores.

(To digress completely, let me take this opportunity to complain about the difference between American comic-book artists and Franco-Belgian comic-book artists. American artists, Carl Barks for example, wrote and drew many classic stories that were on sale for one or two months each, and MIGHT be reprinted years later, with the publisher getting all the revenue. Macherot wrote/drew this one 48-page story for *Spirou* magazine during 1964, it was reprinted as a hardcover cartoon-art novel in 1965, and it has been reprinted ever since, with Macherot getting royalties during his lifetime—I suppose they go to his estate today. Macherot produced many other funny-animal novels during his lifetime, of course, which he got reprint royalties on; Fantagraphics is publishing American editions of them today.)

So animation fans will be watching the progress of *Zootopia* to see whether its plot develops a revolutionary new (for animated movies) story concept, or whether it is just another talking-animal civilization that is just like the human world.

SlashFilm's Russ Fischer reported on August 9, 2013:

> *Tangled* director Byron Howard will direct the film [*Zootopia*] from a script by Jared Bush. They've been working for the last year and a half on the project, spurred in part by a love of the Disney *Robin Hood* feature. Howard wanted to do a film with animals in clothing. They hope to continue "Disney's amazing legacy of animal-based animated films."
>
> [...]
>
> There's also the promise of a unique vision. We've seen movies featuring animals in the natural world, and in the human world, but we've never seen animals in a modern world designed by animals. What would animals do differently than humans would? So the filmmakers talked to experts, from anthropologists to safari guides to imagineers, as they began to design an animal civilization which is "distinctly animal."
>
> In the story, a mountain is an apartment building, and there are "habitats" instead of neighborhoods. Tundratown features polar bear karaoke, and the strange limo/fridge hybrid refrigerzine. Sahara Square is Dubai and Monte Carlo rolled into one, a desert setting, with the Oasis Hotel designed like a palm tree. The Wall Street Gerbil is reading material.
>
> Little Rodencha features tiny streets for rodents; in general, different sizes of animals get, as you'd expect, different sized habitats. Rabbits are in the Burrow Borough, in the Rabbit Transit District. That area has a look influenced by the aesthetic of Studio Ghibli films.

The animals don't always get along, which is a big problem in the city. The conflict can be simplified down to "'flat teeth vs sharp teeth." Nick Wilde, a fox, and Lt. Judy Hopps, a rabbit, begin as natural enemies who evolve into friends by the end of the story.

It does sound promising.

This is really a different subject, but the Japanese TV *Gingitsune* (*Silver Fox*), directed by Misawa Shin (Shin Misawa, American-style; reverse all names here) and produced by Studio Diomedéa, premiered on October 6, 2013, with twelve episodes currently released. The Moetron and Anime News Network websites describe the plot as:

> When her mother passed away at a young age, Saeki Makoto was given the power to see Gintaro, one of the gods' agents that have been protecting the small Inari temple since the Edo era. As only one person of the family can see the fox spirit, Gintaro, naturally as the only blood relative, when her mother passed on, Makoto inherited the sole power to talk to and see him. Although they have their differences, Makoto, with the help of Gintaro's power, help the people of their community deal and solve their problems.

and:

> Makoto is the fifteenth generation heiress of a small shrine to the god Inari. Her father is still the shrine's priest, but Inari's divine messenger, Gintarou, has appeared to Makoto, marking her as true successor. Gintarou has the ability to see a short distance into the future and to find lost objects, but is unmotivated and foulmouthed. In spite of this, he becomes friends with Makoto, and together they help those who come to the shrine.

This series is emphatically for Shinto parishioners, who believe that supernatural animal spirit-gods really do co-exist with humanity, and share the culture of pre-Westernized Japan along with the physical modern Japan. (I was bemused several years ago to find out that there is not only a Shinto god of video recorders, but that there are separate gods for VHS and Betamax recorders. I suppose that there is a god of DVD players today. I can't quite imagine a supernatural anthropomorphized VHS or Betamax player in ancient Japanese society.) I predict that *Gingitsune* will be a massive failure if it is ever brought to America, because there are just not enough Shinto religionists in this country. Anime fans may watch the first two or three episodes to see what it is like, but then they will lose interest, especially if this is a soap opera without much melodrama.

The anime TV series is an adaptation of the manga by Ochiai Sayori, running since 2008. The *Gingitsune* website shows the characters.

Chapter 8

加西生学由天谊 国

Fred Patten Stories

Me & Animation

I often feel a love/hate relationship with Japanese animation. It may be what I am best known for, but it is not the only aspect of animation that I'm interested in. It may be my fault, but I'm more than just "the anime guy".

The first animation that I can remember seeing was when my mother took me to see Disney's *Pinocchio*. *Pinocchio* was released on February 7, 1940, about ten months before I was born, so what I remember must have been the first re-release in October 1945. I remember a bit better the second re-release in February 1954. I was just 13, and my grand-mother took me and my younger sisters to see it at the Mesa Theater, about a mile from home. I loved it so much that I persuaded her to let me stay alone to watch it a second time, and walk home alone afterward.

Of course, there were all of the Disney movies inbetween. *Make Mine Music* and *Song of the South* and *Fun and Fancy Free* and *Melody Time* and *So Dear to My Heart* and *The Adventures of Ichabod and Mister Toad* and *Cinderella* and *Treasure Island* and *Alice in Wonderland* and the re-re-leases of older features like *Fantasia* and *Dumbo* during that time. But all America went to see Disney. When did I become an animation fan?

The first Japanese animated features, *Magic Boy* and *Panda and the Magic Serpent* and *Alakazam the Great*, came to America in June and July 1961, while I was in college. I saw them all. UCLA had occasional programs of "International Animation" on campus. I remember seeing the July 1962 Japanese film *The Adventures of Sinbad* at one of them.

My memory has failed on just how it happened, but somebody invited me to a series of Friday night cartoon screenings at the Hollywood home of Bob Konikow. These ran from about 1970 to 1973. The atten-dance was from a dozen to twenty people, crowded into a darkened living room to watch 16mm prints of whatever the attendees owned or could borrow or check out of a studio's film library. Mark Kausler and Milt Gray usually ran the projector. I saw Victor Haboush's *K-9000: A Space Oddity* and Disney's July 1943 *Victory Through Air Power* here. Jack Warner's personal print of Bob Clampett's *Coal Black and de Sebben Dwarfs* was shown by popular demand at almost every other meeting. I still don't know why I was invited, because all the other attendees seemed to be either young professional animators (with an occasional visit by a "legend" like Bob Clampett or Frank Tashlin) or a published underground cartoonist. Bill Stout, Dave Stevens, John Pound, George DiCaprio, Robert Williams, Bill Spicer, Richard Kyle, Tim Walker, Art Vitello, John Bruno, Bob Foster, and others. The screenings ended when Bob Konikow moved away from Los Angeles, but by then I considered myself an animation insider.

It was at the cartoon screenings at Bob Konikow's that I met Richard Kyle. It turned out that we both were interested in high-quality comic books and newspaper strips from beyond the U.S., and were disappointed that the American comics fanzines only cared about current costumed-hero stuff. Kyle and I decided to go into partnership in opening a specialty comics bookshop, and ordering the best comic art from around the world. This was Graphic Story Bookshop, which opened in January 1972. Shop rentals were cheaper in Long Beach, where Kyle lived, so that was where we rented our first store, in the heart of downtown Long Beach. Kyle ran the shop during the day, and I wrote in the evenings to publishers in Belgium, France, Great Britain, Italy, Japan, the Netherlands, Spain, and West Germany to order their best comics. We sold them mainly through a magazine that Kyle published, *Graphic Story Magazine*, which I wrote book reviews for and made up the advertising copy.

After a couple of years, we realized that the bookshop (which we had renamed Wonderworld Books) was only making enough money for one person to live on. So I stuck to my day job and sold out my half of the partnership to Kyle in December 1975, and became just a steady customer there until Kyle closed the shop in 1996. Still, it was due to being connected with the bookshop that I discovered Japanese animation, and met the fans who helped to start anime fandom in 1977. And it was because of my "professional interest" in Japanese anime and manga that I met Osamu Tezuka when he visited Los Angeles in December 1977. Graphic Story Bookshop may have had only a short direct influence on my life, but it led to a dramatic change that has lasted and grown to the present.

I was also active in science fiction fandom and comic-book fandom. The former led me to discover Japanese manga at a s-f convention in 1970 (which was how I knew to order them for Graphic Story Bookshop), and then anime. I co-founded the first American anime fan club, the Cartoon/Fantasy Organization, in May 1977 (it's still meeting every month). In 1980, I got the Comic-Con's Inkpot Award for introducing anime to American fandom. Toei Animation's Hollywood representative, Pico Hozumi, and TV producer Jim Terry, who was trying to sell an American production of Toei's TV giant-robot animation, provided me with lots of graphics to write articles for popular-culture magazines like *Starlog* on anime. This led to my writing enough articles over the next 25 years to fill a book, *Watching Anime, Reading Manga: 25 Years of Essays and Reviews* (Stone Bridge Press, September 2004).

Anime also got me into the biggest fight that I have ever been in, with Bill Scott of *Rocky and Bullwinkle* fame, at the meetings of ASIFA-Hollywood. Scott dismissed Japanese animation as unimaginative costumed-hero stuff, in horribly limited animation. I rebutted, "You should talk! *Rocky and Bullwinkle* may be brilliant, but it's hardly for the quality of its animation. You have it animated at one of the cheapest studios in Mexico City. As for the giant-robot stereotype, there's much more variety in Japanese animation than there is in American animation. It's that the anime fans don't want to watch anything besides giant robots." But it was a lost cause. I was drowned out by Scott and the other American animation-industry veterans chanting, "Poor animation! Awful animation!" I dropped out of ASIFA-Hollywood for several years.

My record as a comics-fandom fanzine writer-publisher got me a job with Fantagraphics Books' *Amazing Heroes* magazine. My most memorable moment was when I got press credentials to cover a press conference on Ralph Bakshi's *Cool World*, which was just finishing production. There were about a dozen in the press party. We were given a tour of the busy animation studio, set up in a rented warehouse, and then Bakshi came out to say a few words about how imaginative *Cool World* was and how confident the producers were that it would be a hit. Any questions? A big man immediately asked how many cels had been made for the movie, and what arrangements had been made to sell them through a collectibles gallery? Ralph tried to steer the conversation back to *Cool World* as cinematic art, but the guy insisted on asking about the commercial market for the cels, as though the movie was just a ploy to manufacture saleable movie memorabilia. You could see Ralph fighting to keep his temper.

My article on *Cool World* appeared in the final issue of *Amazing Heroes*, #204, in July 1992.

In January 1991, I became the first employee of Carl Macek's and Jerry Beck's Streamline Pictures, turning my anime hobby into my profession. I worked at Streamline until it closed its doors, in March 2002. I became a freelance writer, writing lots of articles for magazines and books on animation, including contributing significant portions of two books by Jerry Beck: *Animation Art: From Pencil to Pixel, the World of Cartoon, Anime, and CGI* (Flame Tree Publishing, August 2004) and *The Animated Movie Guide* (Chicago Review Press, October 2005). At the time I had the stroke in March 2005 that ended my professional animation writing career, I had three monthly columns on anime and manga, in *Animation World Magazine, Comics Buyer's Guide*, and *Newtype U.S.A.* Since then, I have been semi-paralyzed in bed in a convalescent hospital, communicating with the world on a MacBook Pro laptop that I type on with one finger of my left hand. It's enough to let me write weekly columns for Cartoon Research and to review animation books for the online Animation World Network.

Sanrio and Me

Sanrio Co., Ltd. was founded in Japan in August 1960 as the Yamanashi Silk Company, by Shintaro Tsuji, to design, manufacture, and sell "cute" wearing apparel. In April 1973, the company changed its name to Sanrio and began aggressively marketing girls' and women's products. *Hello Kitty* was created in 1974 for little girls' merchandise, followed quickly by *The Little Twin Stars, Tuxedo Sam* (a cute cartoon penguin), *Sugarbunnies, Keroppi* (a cute cartoon frog), and others. Sanrio did not hesitate to license similar foreign goods, becoming the Japanese licensee of Hallmark greeting cards and the *Peanuts* characters of Charles Schulz.

In the late 1970s, Sanrio expanded into girls' manga/comic book publishing and theatrical animation production. In November 1976, it launched *Lyrica*, a monthly comic magazine of almost 200 pages. While all other Japanese manga were printed in monochrome (they often varied signatures printed in different colored inks, offering sections of blue-and-white, green-and-white, black-and-white, purple-and-white, etc., in the same issue), *Lyrica* was in full color. Standard girls' romance stories were mixed with stories featuring *Hello Kitty* and other exclusive Sanrio characters. Sanrio commissioned Osamu Tezuka, one of the most prestigious manga artists in Japan, to create and draw the adventures of a cute cartoon character that it could use in merchandising; this was *Unico*, a baby unicorn. Another feature in *Lyrica* was a lush comic-book serial featuring the fantasy characters from *Metamorphoses*, a theatrical animated feature then in production that Sanrio advertised would be the Japanese equivalent of Disney's *Fantasia*, drawn by one of *Metamorphoses'* animation crew, Don Morgan.

Actually, Sanrio had commissioned *Metamorphoses* to be produced in Hollywood by an experienced American animation staff, directed by Takashi (an artiste; he only used his first name) Yanase. He had been the character designer of Mushi Productions' ambitious 1969 erotic theatrical feature *A Thousand and One Nights*, directed by Osamu Tezuka; one of the longest animated features ever made, at two hours and eleven minutes. *Metamorphoses* was a 70mm adaptation of five of Ovid's Roman tales ("Actaeon", "Orpheus and Eurydice", "Perseus", "The House of Envy", and "Phaëton") with cute cartoon characters and a pop-rock score orchestrated from original rock tunes commissioned for the movie by such big-name composers as Mick Jagger from the Rolling Stones, Joan Baez, and the Pointer Sisters. It ran for 89 minutes. At the same time, Sanrio planned to publish an American version of *Lyrica*, a young girls' comic book in full color (painted watercolor, not the four-screen overlay with dot patterns commonly used for comic book coloring then) of more than 100 pages, with original stories by American comic-book writers and artists, not translations of the Japanese *Lyrica* stories.

In fact, Sanrio held press conferences in America during early 1978 to announce that they planned to take over the American comic-book industry and the moribund theatrical animation industry. Sanrio had already commissioned one animated feature, *The Mouse and His Child*, from the Murakami-Wolf studio, released on November 18, 1977, and a live-action feature, *Who Are the DeBolts? And Where Did They Get Nineteen Kids?*, from Korty Films, released on December 5, 1977. The latter was the winner of four awards, including the 1978 Oscar for Best Documentary Feature, which must have bolstered Sanrio's self-confidence. *Metamorphoses* was to be their first major American release, and they had plans for lots more. *Lyrica* would be their first comic book, a revolutionary magazine that would prove that comics could be much more than the slender pamphlets of the existing American model.

I did not know this. I got involved in it by accident. I was already a rabid Tezuka fan, so when I heard in early 1977 that Tezuka had just created a new full-color comic called *Unico*, serialized in a girls' manga magazine published by Sanrio, which by coincidence had just opened a girls' shop called Gift Gate in nearby Gardena, I hurried there to see if they had it. They did; the first few issues of *Lyrica*. I bought them, and I returned to Gift Gate every month to get the future issues, not just for *Unico*, but for a beautiful fairy-tale strip called *Metamorphoses* by an American artist, Don Morgan.

A couple of months later, a friend told me that some Japanese executives had come to Los Angeles and were planning to publish a new comic book for girls, *Lyrica*. Since I was probably the only American to have ever heard of *Lyrica*, maybe I could present myself as a marketing expert to them and at least get some free samples. It seemed worth a try, so I made an appointment with what turned out to be a Sanrio editorial office. I had hardly opened my mouth when I realized that they thought that I was a professional comic-book writer come to propose a feature for their American *Lyrica*. This was too good an opportunity to pass up, so I made another appointment to return in a week with some story ideas to offer them. They bought two ideas, and hired me to develop one, a s-f story about a young princess of a post-atomic barbarian kingdom, into a 60-page serial at $60 a page. They would hire an artist to draw it.

For the rest of 1977 and early 1978, I spent my spare time divided between the C/FO anime fan club and hanging around Sanrio's rented executive office. *Angela*, my story, was being drawn by Doug Wildey, the writer/artist of the Western newspaper strip *Ambler* and comic-book *Rio*, and creator and writer of *Jonny Quest* for Hanna-Barbera. Sanrio was paying him $120 a page to draw it, which included watercolor-painting each page since *Lyrica* was to be printed in full color. Mark Evanier, who was writing a serial about a teenaged girl 19th-century Mississippi riverboat captain, said that my sale of *Angela* qualified me to join a club of professional comic-book and magazine writers and cartoonists living in the Los Angeles area, the Comic Art Professional Society. I did, and I am still a member, although I've only written a couple of comic-book stories since then. Evanier's story, *Riverboat*, was being drawn by Dan Spiegle. The prolific Evanier had also sold them *The Time Twisters*, drawn by Pat Boyette, and *Keystone*, drawn by Will Meugniot. Dave "Rocketeer" Stevens was there; he was drawing a s-f story that he may have written himself. Evanier vaguely remembers stories that others were doing: something about an Indian brave, drawn by Rick Hoppe, and something drawn by Willie Ito, a veteran Hanna-Barbera cartoonist. One that was turned down was *Queen Cutlass*, about a female pirate captain in a sword-&-sorcery world, by writer Don Glut and artist Rick Hoberg. The Sanrio editors didn't like it.

As time went on, I and most of the American comics professionals got the increasing impression that the Sanrio executives were out of touch with the reality of the American comic-book industry. The 100+ page *Lyrica* could not be printed by any regular comics printer. It would have to cost a *lot* more than the then-standard 15¢. It would presumably contain advertising for Sanrio's merchandise for girls, which would particularly turn away any boys who might otherwise buy it. Would it fit onto newsstands (comics specialty shops were just beginning) along with other comic books? What would the regular newsstand distributors think of such an oddball comic book? They had recently killed Martin Goodman's 1974-75 attempt to create a new line of Atlas Comics, by declining to distribute them because they felt that the comics racks were already too crowded. The Sanrio executives casually dismissed all these concerns, saying, "We will take care of that. You just do what we are paying you to do." We shrugged and, as the saying goes, "took the money and ran".

We could not help hearing about Sanrio's other big project, to create a theatrical animated "modern *Fantasia*". Sanrio had set up a fully-staffed animation studio nearby, and some of the animators occasionally visited the Sanrio offices. Don Morgan, who was drawing the *Metamorphoses* strip in the Japanese *Lyrica*, was a layout artist on the film. The animators had allied concerns. Some of the animation did not make any story sense. The animation had nothing to do with the music, which was often too short or too long for the scene. One scene had the Boy walking and walking and walking and walking, for no reason other than to "use up" all the music. Some said bluntly that Takashi had been named the director only because he was from Japan, unlike the Anglos and the Japanese Nisei and Sansei born and raised in America. Everyone complained that he did not know what he was doing, but would not admit it. Again, the Sanrio executives said, "Don't worry about it. Just animate like we're paying you to do."

Metamorphoses premiered to great fanfare in NYC on May 3, 1978. If it wasn't the biggest bomb in cinematic history, it was close. The animation was smooth and rich, but B-O-R-I-N-G! If the story were any more arty/intellectual, it would have been condescending. The reviews were not kind.

An article in *Business Week*, May 22, 1978, when Sanrio still had hopes for the movie, reported:

> Entertainment: A JAPANESE COURTSHIP OF THE DISNEY AUDIENCE.
>
> Critical reaction to *Metamorphoses*, a glossy animated film on Greek mythology that hit U.S. movie houses last week, has not lived up to the $6 million, three-year effort the movie represents. Billed as a successor to Walt Disney's *Fantasia*, the rock-music cartoon is "about as interesting as wallpaper," says *The Los Angeles Times*.
>
> But if *Metamorphoses* proves a dud, it is nonetheless a significant step for its producer, Japan's Sanrio Co. The first major theatrical film produced in Hollywood by a Japanese company, it is the kickoff of a $50 million drive by Sanrio to become "a major force in U.S. filmmaking," says the company's founder and president, Shintaro Tsuji. As if taking on Hollywood were not brash enough, Sanrio is also plunging into children's retailing in the U.S. by setting up its

own shops and signing up department stores to handle the 1,800-odd children's products it markets.

SELLING JOY. In Japan, Sanrio is a kind of Japanese Walt Disney, churning out children's magazines, films, and saccharine-sweet cartoon characters that embellish an army of kiddie products from bicycles to chopsticks. All these products are designed to fit an obsessive corporate goal: "We don't want to just make money but to make people feel warm and happy," insists Tsuji. The business of joy pays off, however: Sanrio expects to earn $20 million in sales—mostly in Japan—of $250 million in the fiscal year ending July 31.

To spread happiness, Tsuji plans to invest upwards of $50 million in wholesome Hollywood films—"instead of buying American securities or shopping centers, which has been offered." One immediate problem: No U.S. film distributor would touch *Metamorphoses*. Says one: "It's extremely difficult to market animated films unless you're Disney. They're going to get killed." Undaunted, Tsuji formed his own distribution subsidiary, which has signed up some 50 theaters in Western states to show the film. At the Los Angeles theater where it premiered, it has surprised skeptics by grossing a respectable $26,000 in its first week.

Sanrio has financed two other U.S.-made films—a love-conquers-all documentary about a California family that adopted 15 handicapped children, and a children's cartoon feature called *The Mouse and Its [sic.] Child*. And, to keep his new distribution company in business, Tsuji has also started to acquire ready-made films—of a suitably joyful nature.

BOUTIQUES. Sanrio's U.S. marketing strategy is less risky, but it is also aggressive. Last year the company began lining up retailers to handle its children's items, and it now claims to have nearly 1,500 outlets. Tsuji is pushing department store chains to open boutiques for his products. At the same time, he is starting a U.S. chain of Sanrio children's shops, emulating the 17 Gift Gate stores the company owns in Japan. Two California test stores opened last fall. Tsuji has plans for others in New York, Chicago, and Kansas City; he aims for 10 stores later.

Tsuji sees the U.S. shops mainly as image-building outlets that will let Sanrio test products on the U.S. market before releasing them to department stores. Items it now sells in the U.S. include educational toys, plush animals, and children's greeting cards. The greeting-card business is a big one; Sanrio is the Japanese distributor for Hallmark products.

No stranger to filmmaking, Sanrio has produced eight films in Japan since entering the business there five years ago, and it is a major shareholder in Toho Co., Japan's largest cinema chain. But the company ruled out making movies in Japan for export because Japanese films are generally relegated to art theaters in the U.S. and Europe. If Sanrio's audacious Hollywood venture pays off, Tsuji has big plans for entrenching his company there. He is talking of buying a record company and maybe even a movie studio of his own. [p. 34, with a photograph of Tsuji standing next to a large *Metamorphoses* poster]

I don't know where *Business Week* got the information about screenings in Los Angeles during May. I was invited to an "exclusive premiere screening" at a swanky Century City theater on June 14. The theater was packed, largely with the film's production crew and their families. Each attendee got a fancy press kit with a cover full-color reproduction of the movie's poster showing wild horses galloping out of the ocean's foam, by Western Printing artist Mo Gollub, the painter of many of Western Printing's Gold Key comic book covers. The screening was a special disaster, because in addition to the movie's other problems, the sound track was turned up to full volume. The orchestral pop-rock music was so deafening that it literally drove some of the audience out of the theater. It was rumored that it was so loud that plaster was flaking from the ceiling, while Takashi was complaining, "Can't you turn up the sound any louder?" The lack of dialogue and having the same Boy and Girl as actors portraying the protagonists in each story confused many people. They thought the Boy and Girl were supposed to be the same characters throughout, and "why is the Boy dying over and over again?"

I don't think that *Metamorphoses* was ever shown again. Columbia Pictures had given it a limited release in Los Angeles on the same day, and the comments from the few other theaters that showed it were the same (except for the overly-loud music). It was quickly pulled from release. Nothing was seen for over a year, then in May 1979 it was released in an entirely new form. It was retitled *Winds of Change*; it was cut from 89 minutes to 82 minutes; the arrangement of the five sequences was altered; the Boy was named Wondermaker; the orchestral rock score was completely discarded for a new disco score by Alex Costandinos that was composed to fit the action; and narration by Peter Ustinov was added to explain, often sarcastically, the action. In October, it was released in Japan in a third cut, retitled *Orpheus of the Stars,* with singers Arthur Simms and Pattie Brooks replacing the Rolling Stones. RCA Columbia Pictures Home Video released *Winds of Change* as a "Magic Window" children's video in the 1980s, which was rereleased as a regular home video in January 1992, but no version of *Metamorphoses* is available today.

By this time, the *Lyrica* project was long dead, along with Sanrio's other American filmmaking plans. All that the Sanrio execs would say as they closed their Santa Monica office was, "We have done more market research, and we have decided that the time is not right for a *Lyrica*-type magazine. But you have done what we asked you to do, so you may keep the money." They even gave the artists their stories back to sell elsewhere. (If they could. I know that Doug Wildey complained that no American comic-book publisher was interested in buying a 60-page romantic s-f story designed for young girls.)

I treated my $3,600 ($3,700 including my second idea, which they were going to have me write once *Lyrica* was a success) as a windfall that gave me enough with what I already had to buy a brand-new car. So I can't complain. It would have been nice to see *Angela* printed, though. Doug Wildey's art was excellent.

The Japanese *Lyrica* was discontinued after the March 1979 issue, but surprisingly Sanrio continued to produce animated features, although in Japan for Japanese theatrical distribution. America got them and one live-action feature for TV and home video release in the early 1980s:

- *Ringing Bell*
- *The Glacier Fox* (live-action documentary on arctic foxes)
- *Nutcracker Fantasy* (stop-motion)
- *The Fantastic Adventures of Unico*
- *The Legend of Syrius/Sea Prince and the Fire Child*
- *Unico in the Island of Magic*
- *A Journey Through Fairyland*

Since the early 1980s, Sanrio has concentrated on promoting *Hello Kitty* in theatrical and TV animation to keep awareness of her high for Japanese marketing purposes, and in America on just selling the *Hello Kitty* merchandise. The latter is so widespread throughout America that Sanrio must be "crying all the way to the bank", as Liberace said in another context, about its failure to establish a theatrical or newsstand presence. Around the world, too: there are several *Hello Kitty* restaurants throughout Asia, and even a *Hello Kitty* maternity hospital in Taiwan. But there are no more international or American Sanrio movies. Briefly, though, it felt glorious to be a part of an apparently more-realistic-than-most project to get Japanese animation into America.

About the Author

Fred Patten is a world-renowned historian and author in such fields as anime, manga, animation, and science fiction. In 1972, Fred became co-owner of the Graphic Story Bookshop in Long Beach, California, selling imported manga and comics from Japan, France, and elsewhere, and later he worked for Streamline Pictures, one of the country's first anime production companies. Fred has written regularly for such publications as *Animation World Magazine* and *Comics Buyer's Guide*, and writes a weekly column for the Cartoon Research website.

About the Publisher

Theme Park Press is the largest independent publisher of Disney and Disney-related pop culture books in the world.

Established in November 2012 by Bob McLain, Theme Park Press has released best-selling print and digital books about such topics as Disney films and animation, the Disney theme parks, Disney historical and cultural studies, park touring guides, autobiographies, fiction, and more.

For more information, and a list of forthcoming titles, please visit:

http://themeparkpress.com

More Books from Theme Park Press

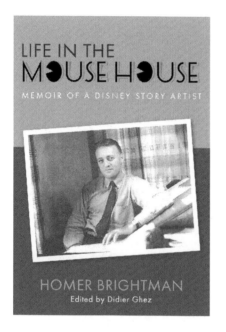

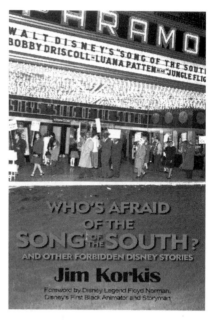

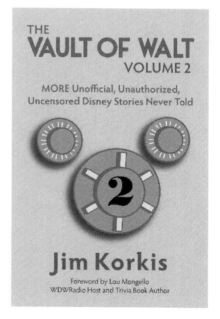

To see all our books, visit ThemeParkPress.com

Index

See the popular abbreviation, not the full title, for example: *Captain Harlock*, not *Space Pirate Captain Harlock*.

Real people are listed by last name, first name: Disney, Walt. Fictitious people are listed by first name followed by last name: Ataru Moroboshi.